THE MAN
WITH THE
CALABASH PIPE

BOOKS BY OLIVER LA FARGE

Tribes and Temples (*with Frans Blom*), 1926–1927

Laughing Boy, 1929

The Year Bearer's People (*with Douglas Byers*), 1931

Introduction to American Indian Art (*with John Sloan*), 1931

Sparks Fly Upward, 1931

Long Pennant, 1933

All the Young Men, 1935

The Enemy Gods, 1937

An Alphabet for Writing the Navajo Language, 1940

As Long as the Grass Shall Grow, 1940

The Changing Indian (*editor*), 1942

The Copper Pot, 1942

War Below Zero (*with Corey Ford and Bernt Balchen*), 1944

Raw Material, 1945

Santa Eulalia, 1947

The Eagle in the Egg, 1949

Cochise of Arizona, 1953

The Mother Ditch, 1954

A Pictorial History of the American Indian, 1956

Behind the Mountains, 1956

A Pause in the Desert, 1957

Sante Fe: The Autobiography of a Southwestern Town (*with Arthur N. Morgan*), 1959

The Door in the Wall, 1965

The Man with the Calabash Pipe (*edited by Winfield Townley Scott*), 1966

THE
MAN
WITH THE
CALABASH PIPE

Some Observations

by

Oliver La Farge

Edited and with
an Introduction by

Winfield Townley Scott

VVVVVVVVVVVVVV

Houghton Mifflin Company Boston

𝕿𝖍𝖊 𝕽𝖎𝖛𝖊𝖗𝖘𝖎𝖉𝖊 𝕻𝖗𝖊𝖘𝖘 𝕮𝖆𝖒𝖇𝖗𝖎𝖉𝖌𝖊

1966

First Printing   W

Printed in the United States of America

ACKNOWLEDGMENT

I wish to thank Mr. Robert M. McKinney, publisher of *The New Mexican*, for his courtesy in permitting the reprinting of the material in this book and to record that he was the first to suggest that a book of this sort should be made. I also wish to thank Eleanor M. Scott, my wife, for her generous cooperation.

It is not my privilege to dedicate another man's writing, but I should like to say that I made this book first of all for Consuelo Baca de La Farge and her son John.

THE EDITOR

Contents

Contents

Introduction

OLIVER LA FARGE in the 1920's and '30's sometimes visited Sante Fe, New Mexico, and for a couple of years in the '30's was a resident of the town, but it was in 1946 that he finally settled here. He was then forty-five. Here he lived the last seventeen years of his life and here he is buried under one of the small identical headstones in the National Cemetery that mark so many hundreds of those who like himself served his country in uniform.

Santa Fe is as foreign to as it is far from New York, where La Farge was born; from Narragansett Bay, for which he kept always a passionate affection as the central scene of his growing up; from Groton, where he went unhappily to school; and from Harvard, where he went happily to college. Yet it was the Southwest to which he first came as a very young anthropologist. Santa Fe is surrounded by the Indian country with which La Farge's largest fame has been connected. And he loved the town itself with a convert's zeal. This book is only partially about Santa Fe, but the reader will find that La Farge scolded, reprimanded, corrected, reminded, berated, bemoaned, rejoiced in, urged on the town in a dozen moods, always out of a fierce devotion. Though often in the background, and with much said relevant to anywhere in America, a strong sense of place permeates these essays, whatever their matter. The Southwest in general, Santa Fe in particular, became his *locus classicus* — or his pulpit.

La Farge once remarked that, as the years went on, the East interested him less and less: he was willing to give back Washington, D.C., to the congressmen, he had begun to doubt that New York is a nice place to visit. "Santa Fe," he summed it up, "has made a rube out of me." That was uncharacteristically inaccurate of Oliver La Farge but it indicates the depth of his identification.

From 1950 until just before his death in August 1963, La Farge wrote a weekly column for the Sunday edition of Santa Fe's daily paper, *The New Mexican.* He rarely missed a Sunday. Sometimes illness prevented briefly, sometimes travel; most often his annual trip back East, principally given over to work for the Association on American Indian Affairs. At a rough guess, the full file runs to 350,000 words. The clippings, with few exceptions, are pasted and dated on sheets of yellow paper, and Consuelo La Farge has confirmed my surmise that he thought he might make use of them in a book. His widow says, "Oliver felt that some of his best material was in the articles and planned some day to pull them together." He was a thrifty Yankee. And I wish he had lived to make such a book. As the succursal substitute, I have attempted to retrieve the best, most representative and generally interesting columns so that La Farge's national audience may have some of his most engaging writing.

Not many months before his death, La Farge wrote a column about his column:

> The editors of that excellent magazine, *The New Mexico Architect*, have paid me the staggering compliment of devoting an editorial to taking me to task for inconsistency in two columns I wrote, one on The Gate of Spain and one on The Palace restaurants. They have further overwhelmed me by inviting me, in print and verbally, to write a rebuttal. And I find myself unable to offer them much more than to say I don't take myself that seriously.

Which leads me to some reflections upon the scope and intent of this column. The original idea was that it was to be largely literary in content, but as editors came and went and time passed, it developed into a general commentary on the local scene. At times it seems to me that I am doing little more than talking to myself in print, but I gather from what I am told that I usually manage to interest or amuse some readers, which is all I can ask. Of course, I do not often hear from the ones who think I stink, and I have no way of knowing how many they may be.

I am not an authority on much of anything. I am a citizen, and a resident of Santa Fe, and as such entitled to my opinions. So long as *The New Mexican* thinks it worth while to print certain of these opinions on Sundays, I shall provide the copy. It is a good deal of fun, tempered by the obligation to be responsible, which does not mean always to be serious or even to pontificate.

As a young man, I was exposed to an excellent, although now old-fashioned, liberal education. Some of it took. My major study was anthropology, in which I received a master's degree, and which I practiced professionally, at the desk and in the field, for some years. Since I achieved status as a writer, however, my contact with the science has been as an amateur.

I have had the good fortune to have travelled fairly widely, although superficially. With the lapse of time, I have become an old resident of Santa Fe, with an interested layman's knowledge, no more, of the city's history and traditions. Like most even medium old-timers, I have had a good deal of contact, mostly informal and unorganized, with the Indians of this general vicinity. I speak Spanish fairly fluently, inaccurately, and with a bad accent.

During the past thirty years, after my writing, my chief interest has been in the present condition, problems, and advancement of the Indians of the United States, what is loosely known as "Indian Affairs." This has led to such unexpected developments as exchanging correspondence with Eskimos.

I prefer to keep Indian affairs out of my column for various reasons, one of which is that I have grown weary of listening to myself on the subject.

Above are listed the qualifications, or lack of qualifications, of this casual columnist. Perhaps I should add, although it is clearly inferred above, that I am first and foremost a professional, free-lance writer, which is relevant to writing columns.

If possible, I should like my columns to be good-natured, unless I am greatly worked up over something important, which is not often. I want to avoid being shrill. I try to write about things that I think people want discussed, and I include politics and such matters although I am no politician or professional commentator. The column is subjective, that is, it expresses my opinion, an opinion formed about the way any of us who are not authorities form our opinions.

Above all, I don't delude myself that my remarks are important, although on some occasions I hope that what I write may help to form or strengthen or crystallize public opinion. It has been quite clear to me that on many occasions I have wielded no such influence. That the column will be inconsistent is inevitable, and bothers me not in the least.

From time to time I receive telephone calls, or letters, from complete strangers, or encounter them somewhere, who tell me that they like my column. So long as the line I am following, erratic and undirected though it may be, brings me that pleasure, I shall continue to follow it.

I suspect, although La Farge was paid for the job, that his column was a busman's holiday. It was a weekly assignment which he could fulfill with the ease of a local audience. Naturally many columns date or stay too intimately local for further consumption; yet once I put all such aside there was still a considerable task to bring down to a moderate-sized book so much that remains lively. He frequently returned to certain preoccupations and so, here, I have often been able to weld several columns together and avoid the staccato effect of identically lengthed pieces and thus make full-fledged what was originally a scattering of observations.

Of course that sardonic *alter ego*, The Man with the Calabash Pipe, has to remain intermittent because his appearance on the scene is staged with deliberate (and charming) repetitiousness. La Farge used him frequently and I have had to just let him come and go. I only wish there were more of his delightful Indian counterpart, Horned Husband Kachina Chief, whose brief appearances emphasize that in this book we get the humorous play of Oliver La Farge's mind as in no other book of his.

It was an extraordinary mind. I have come upon a remark La Farge made about a famed anthropologist, A. L. Kroeber: "the possessor of a mind capable of incredible storage and constantly beautiful illumination." That describes La Farge's own. Whenever I was with him — and I was with him uncounted times for nearly a decade — I felt the deference one should feel to that rare person who keeps the possession of a rich education and a great facility in the employment of it. Here is the essential reason that a book such as this can be drawn from a seemingly casual Sunday column. Again and again La Farge takes off from an event in his own life or in his town or in the world and proceeds from the particular to the general significance. Or as William Maxwell once so well put it in commenting on what he called La Farge's polemical writing: "Clarity, a wide knowledge, incorruptible fairness, intellectual movement, and literary grace all illuminated and transformed his argument. As naturally as breathing, he moved away from the immediate situation to the general one, from the smaller explanation to the larger."

My personal joy in this book is in having his voice instruct-

ing me yet again. And I think any reader who never had the
luck to know Oliver La Farge will touch the man as nowhere
else in his work save perhaps that revealing autobiography,
Raw Material; and will be touched and will come to feel the
overtones of a unique, complex individual.

He was not easy to know, nor in all the years I regarded him
with affection as well as admiration could I quite lose a wari-
ness in his presence. He was a man of fierce pride. He seemed
to me to be a creature whose sensibilities were so fine that I
feared those of us with blunter sensibilities might, however
unintentionally, outrage or offend or hurt him. Or, at the
least, disappoint him.

My friendship with him began with my own settling in Santa
Fe in 1954. But I had once met him for an hour or so, probably in 1947, at the home of the architect Alexander Knox
in Saunderstown, Rhode Island. I had some acquaintance
with his writing brother, Christopher La Farge, but I had come
to the Knox house as a working newspaperman to do a brief
interview. Chiefly I recall being struck by the dark, exotic
beauty of his wife Consuelo who, as readers of *Behind the
Mountains* know, is a distinguished mix of French and Spanish. She looked foreign on the shores of Narragansett Bay, but
then in a way so did La Farge himself: his lean frame, his
handsome bony face, his brown skin and very dark hair — he
looked rather Indian, some of whose blood in fact he did have
intermingled with Hazard and Perry and Lockwood and La
Farge. Of the interview I recall nothing save that when I in-
quired what he did about swimming in Santa Fe he replied,
"You cultivate friends who have swimming pools."

Of course he was not in the least foreign in New England.
An accident of reputation, arising from his writing about and
working for the American Indian, tended to obscure for many
people the basic character: La Farge first of all was a New

England Yankee, a proud Yankee, an aristocratic Yankee. And although he was born in New York he sometimes referred to Rhode Island — as the reader will find in this book — as "my native state." From the Newport side of the Bay to the Saunderstown side, there was his ancestry, there were his roots, his most beloved memories and his lifelong loyalties.

He loved talking about it all with a fellow New Englander. He loved coming to my house for the Rhode Island jonny cakes which my wife would cook for him — the white corn- meal imported from "back home." When our men's club, *Quien Sabe,* formed for eating and drinking and conversation, met at La Farge's he would serve his specialty, fish chowder. He was fond of telling Yankee anecdotes — with an exagger- ated dialect. As a sample of his devotion, I remember his saying, very seriously, "Why is it that on that sparse New England soil they can raise corn that makes all other corn taste as though you were chewing somebody else's gums?"

Nor shall I ever forget the last time I was with him. I drove him to his house on College Street at the end of an afternoon we had spent as participants in a public panel discussion on civic beauty and ugliness. He looked alarmingly exhausted but when he insisted I come in for a drink I went in. And he relaxed and began to look better and we had a good time as always. I had recently returned from a vacation in Rhode Island's South County, and I talked of that; it was especially his country, and as he and Consuelo were seeing me to the door I said, "You can't imagine how often I thought of you while I was there — how often I thought 'Oliver would like to see that.'" He said nothing. He glowed. And for the first time in our near-decade of friendship for an instant he threw an arm around my shoulders. Just for an instant, of course: where we came from, one doesn't overdo that sort of gesture.

As in this book, he loved to talk about dozens of things.

"Ask Oliver a question and you get a dissertation," remarked one friend — not unfondly. Well, he was a good talker, whether the subject was New England or Indians, anthropology or politics. He was testy. He strove for exactitude in what he said and how he said it. He held opinions strongly — and if you disagreed he could marshall his facts dismayingly. For example, I think there is a lot of what can be termed "regional writing" which is at once minor and very valuable; but I never could get him to regard "regional writing" as anything but a dirty epithet.

Perhaps above all, given a congenial audience, he liked to discuss writing. Allegedly stolid Indians from the pueblos of Taos, Tesuque, Santa Clara, stood weeping beside La Farge's open grave. His obituaries across the country gave prominence to his work for the American Indian, rather to the slighting of his literary work. But eventually we must see and assess La Farge as a writer. Public service, however honorable, is a temporary thing; it may leave a "lasting effect," yet that will be enclosed in history as writing is not.

In the Foreword to the Sentry Edition of _Laughing Boy_, La Farge, speaking so movingly of the remote young man who had written the book, mused over how astonished he would have been could he have known that after thirty years the novel was still in print, still being read. "But there is no way to reach back and tell him that, and it probably is better that he did the thing for itself, because he had to, and for no other reason. That leaves the gratification to me, his successor, who am much older and much more in need of encouragement." Those are the remarks of an artist.

There he touched, however gently, the nerve that seared him. He had had that terrible misfortune of immediate success unmatched by his later work. Despite three prolific decades he was known as "the author of _Laughing Boy_." Some admirers of that book — as readers of *The Man with the Calabash Pipe* will discover — were even unaware that he had written anything else at all. He hoped and there must have been times when he knew — what was true — that there was maturer, finer writing in several of the later books and in many of the short stories. But the wound was there and it was deep. Friends learned to say little or nothing to him about *Laughing Boy*. Nevertheless among friends he sometimes gave voice to the blackest bitterness, excoriated "junk" he had written, and he bent under the self-accusation of "just an old has-been." Such naked despair was infrequent yet it must be reported in any attempt to suggest the complexities of a man whose normal humor was one of cheerful seriousness. He could be a tough *hombre* in his demands on others as on himself, but his skin was thin.

The American middle class being the vast sprawling mass which it is, most of our artists of all kinds emerge from it. Our slums and our palatial homes rarely produce any artists of importance. I don't imply the La Farges lived in palaces. But the family tree for generations was filled with people of distinction and fame in the field of the arts, most notably the grandfather, John La Farge, painter, stained-glass designer, and close friend of many eminent men of the 19th century. The family "connections" — to use that slightly snobbish but inevitable and valid word — were always of the best. It would be John La Farge, for instance, who in Newport was the first to encourage young Henry James to continue with his writing. And I recall what someone said years ago of Oliver's brother Christopher: someone said that if Christopher wasn't exactly born with a silver spoon in his mouth, nonetheless there was a lot of fine old heirloom silver lying around handy.

Now this aristocratic heritage — for it really is that, and in American society from the Adams family on we really possess such a thing — can have its strictures, its handicaps for the creative person. He is born to a Name, he has something "to live up to."

In *Raw Material* La Farge prods at the dichotomy of genteel tradition and artistic heritage. Within the Groton School tradition, he says, "I was particularly prone to aspirations toward conservative gentility which actually were alien to my make-up; to live uptown in a presentable apartment, have friends out of the same drawer as myself, give dinners of six and eight deftly served, accompanied by the right wines, and to be asked to the small, fashionable parties (white tie) — a death in life, which I eagerly embraced as soon as financial success enabled me to, and of which it took a series of disasters to cure me."

(This was just after the publication of *Laughing Boy* and his first marriage in 1929. The southwestern writer, Mary Austin, impressed by that novel, sought out La Farge in New York, took one look around that uptown, presentable apartment, and said "Well, I never expected to find *you* in a place like *this!*" So he once told me.)

Further in *Raw Material* he speaks of the "great disadvantage to be born a La Farge and have gone to Groton. . . . The pressure to do the kind of writing only a gentleman would do, to be, God help me, in good taste, was terrific, and the Groton boy of course insisted on it. It cost me a constant struggle to write the thing as I saw it, and on many occasions I failed. Only recently have I really unloaded this influence. . . . It is only recently that I have been able to eliminate the fatal consideration of whether a given piece of writing would be, not only artistically sound, but creditable to myself."

I think he remained a mixture — partly as a writer and always as a man — of East Coast and Southwest, of Groton-Harvard breeding and hard-eyed artist. As he said, his grandfather John "was a gentleman in his ordinary converse because he was bred that way, but as far as I can find out, when he painted he painted, and to hell with everything." Oliver La Farge had some triumphs and an honored name in the world, and he had some dissatisfactions and disappointments. It may be that the intensity of his character throve on the conflict of his inheritance.

The intensity was always there: La Farge, dashing in blue neckerchief, riding a beautiful horse in Santa Fe's Fiesta parade; or, Astrakhan hat on head in winter, peering into a First Grade window of Acequia Madre School — quite alarming to the teacher — to see what was going on in his son Pen's class (John Pendaries, known as "Pen"); or instituting a regularity of afternoon tea for Pen's refinement; or rushing home late for the cocktail hour because — with as much pride as though it were the Harvard crew — he had been watching Pen playing Little League baseball; or plunging white-faced to the barricade at the Santa Fe Rodeo when his older son Peter had been thrown from a bronco. And always the talk — learned, flowing, emphatic, uncompromising.

Thomas Wentworth Higginson, writing from Newport nearly a century ago, said, "I ought not to complain of living in a place which has John La Farge. . . . He is one of the few men to whom it is delightful to talk — almost the only one with whom I can imagine talking all night." In a far and different town many of us felt just like that about John La Farge's distinguished, unforgettable grandson. In this book alone, the sound and the illumination of his talk are preserved.

W. T. S.

Santa Fe, New Mexico

I

*Around and
About a City*

The Man with
the Calabash Pipe: I

WITH THE LAST of the holidays, including two birthday parties, just behind me, I relaxed in an armchair, feeling somewhat depleted. At this juncture my very learned friend, the Man with the Calabash Pipe, dropped in, bringing with him a package of fine, mild pipe tobacco and a bottle of excellent sherry, surpluses from his Christmas take. He is a bachelor; he lives in a house that is always in need of housekeeping; he has the look of one who could do with the touch of a woman's hand, preferably wielding a clothes brush and a curry comb; and, as a result, women shower the poor lonely fellow with gifts.

It is something of a racket, and I told him so, adding, "Which makes you the only man I know whose badly-tied tie is functional."

"That's all very well," he said, pulling the cork from the bottle, "but at least I'm not pooped by the holidays. Look at you."

"You've probably stayed in bed all morning for the last week."

He looked guilty.

"I admit, I can't take it as once I did. When I was a roaring young blade at college, I came to New York for Christmas, hardly able to wait to get to the first dance. We went to one or two parties every night, except on Christmas day itself, made dates in the daytime, and returned to our studies feeling refreshed."

I went and got glasses.

"And," said my friend, "if what your brother has told me is correct, after a Christmas Eve debutante ball you dragged yourselves from bed moaning, in order to greet your quiet-living parents, went through church in something of a daze, and fell upon the noon-day eggnog as pure medicine."

"But the next day we were up with a bounce."

"Yes. That kind of thing is for the young. For the next fifteen years — if by chance you last that long — you can just relax and let your child do the going for you. Of course, you will get up early for his sake, and a little later he will feel called upon to get up early for your sake, and by and by you will stop fooling each other, but leave it to youth." He raised his glass, "Here's to this fresh, untried New Year."

After he had sipped, he sighed faintly. "Youth," he said. "Youth. Age thinks, frets, considers; youth acts. The kids got their snow. You worried about the ranchers out in the country and whether you could get to the garage to have chains put on. To your child, the snow was something to do something about, and promptly."

I nodded.

"You can't help the ranchers by sitting behind the window and worrying about them. You can't do them any harm by building a snow man. The child never lets himself be deterred by the academic."

He filled his pipe. "To a child, not only snow, but most phenomena of nature, are to be accepted as they come and promptly put to use. This applies to mud, sand, water, trees, long grass, small stones, rocks, soft asphalt, and wet cement. A sound resolution for the old codgers like you for this still shiny New Year would be to evaluate less and enjoy more."

He paused to light up.

"I suppose," I said, "that you went out and made a snow man last week?"

"We-ell, no. I watched out the window. Vicarious pleasures can be delightful."

I tried the sherry; it was of the best. "And the moral of this little sermon of yours?"

"It has none." He looked at me with a faint smile. "In your decrepit condition you'll never think up a column, so, if you wish, you may quote me."

And I have.

New Mexico and Santa Fe

THIS ENTERPRISING metropolitan daily has recently been running a distinctly hair-raising study of popular opinion of New Mexico among people of the more distant states. That is, hair-raising if you haven't recently travelled beyond the borders of the states that neighbor us and sampled common opinion for yourself, or kept track of the reports from time to time of those firms that still think New Mexico is a foreign nation and offer to quote local customers prices in pesos.

It will take a very high grade public education campaign, something well beyond the mere taking of ads and considerably more deeply conceived, to disabuse the mass of the American public from the ideas that:

A. New Mexico is a flat, arid desert.

B. Its climate is hot in winter, unbearably hot in summer.

C. Its largest centers of population consist of a handful of mud huts with, perhaps, a few wigwams on the outskirts.

D. It and its inhabitants are not really American and are dirty and dangerous, and

E. There is nothing on earth to see or do there.

Good and accurate books by people who knew and loved New Mexico have been being published and selling well for nearly fifty years. Magazine articles about the state appear constantly (for which local writers should be thankful). Those who have really visited the state, and not merely hurried through it on Route 66, must number in the millions by now. Still the ignorance persists.

Part of the delusion about New Mexico arises from what would seem to be the logical reasoning that, if the middle western states are so perfectly awful in summer, an arid state on the Mexican border must be worse.

One time I attended a wedding in St. Louis in July. The muggy heat was pure murder. With deep relief I climbed on the train, which was moderately air-conditioned, looking forward eagerly to my return to cool New Mexico.

On the train were two young ladies, registered nurses specializing in polio, from, I believe, Minnesota and Michigan. They were being sent to Albuquerque, and were going in a spirit of sheer heroism. I soon learned that they looked forward with dread to the even greater heat and the loneliness and dreariness of life in a village of mud huts.

I did mention that it was a pity they weren't being sent to Santa Fe, but chiefly I went about relieving their fears. I told them that Albuquerque had traffic lights (that was just before they were installed here). I described the readily accessible mountain country, and explained what relatively high altitudes and dry air meant in terms of cool nights. It seemed kinder not to say anything about dust.

It was all news to them. So was the size of that city and of Santa Fe, and the choice of hotels available when they should visit the pleasanter, older city. They were also greatly relieved to know that everyone except a few elderly Indians and a very few old natives living in the most remote, back country, spoke English. I am happy to say that they did know that New Mexico was a part of the United States.

Their relief was tremendous. For a clincher, I asked whether they would be in the state through the winter, and when they said they would be, told them to send for their skiing equipment. That, as I have found before, was the real punch line.

Why is it that, with all the free advertising in print and by word of mouth that this state has had for nearly fifty years, the ignorance still persists? Everybody knows what, for instance, Massachusetts is like. Why should we be the victims of a lot of pure folklore?

I don't know the answers, but I do believe that we can't cure our condition simply by paid advertising in the usual sense of the word. We need, as I said at the beginning, a thoroughly thought through campaign of public education. Once everyone in the United States knows what New Mexico is like, everyone will come here, and we of New Mexico, in turn, to save our lives can pull up stakes and take over New England.

When I was young and bumptious, I used to declare that I would live only in a really big city, such as London, Paris, or New York, or in a village. This reflected the narrowness of my experiences. I had grown up partly in New York, and partly in a metropolis of some three hundred houses known as Saunderstown, R.I. In college years I came to know Boston. Boston is a unique town. Unique is derived from the Latin words *unus*, "one," and *equus*, "horse."

Fate landed me in New Orleans, a small city by a New Yorker's standards, but a thoroughly delightful one. So I made an exception, conscious that New Orleans is also unique, unusually rich in character, unusually equipped with charm. I still held to the opinion that, by and large, small cities and smaller towns were drab and dreadful places.

Now it is getting to be a good many years since first I settled in Santa Fe, perched, in a spirit of inquiry and doubt, in a rented house, and the longer I live here, regretfully seeing the population pass the 30,000 mark, the better I like it. A small town has warmth and rewards that big city dwellers never dream of.

To some extent, New Mexico, a sparsely settled state, partakes of the same advantages. In both state and town, politics are live, the major personalities really alive to us. The percentage of voters who actually know the candidates is much higher, which makes the whole business much more real.

In decades of voting residence in New York, I never knew the mayor, an alderman, a governor, congressman, or senator. Now as I start counting, I find I have had some acquaintance with every New Mexico senator and congressman, with the exception of Mrs. Lusk, since Albert Simms, Bronson Cutting, and Samuel Bratton. I have also at least met every governor since Arthur Seligman, whom I remember with affection.

Few New Yorkers even think of attending a meeting of the city council; few Santa Feans would hesitate for a moment to do so if any matter of interest to them was coming up. Life in a small town and in a state of small population is a life among real people; life in a big city is life among impersonal names.

In New York, one's friends live scattered over a fairly large area, made larger in its effect by the congestion of unknowns and the complexities of getting from here to there. As a usual thing, one is careful not to strike up an acquaintance with people who live in the same building, since that could be a real nuisance.

We lived for a year and a half on 10th Street between Fifth and Sixth Avenues. I suppose each of us must have walked the length of that block at least once a day. In an unreal way, we became acquainted with the neighboring merchants — not as one would in Santa Fe, where one shares so many more interests than the mere commercial transaction. But we could walk that block day after day forever without exchanging a greeting with anyone, without encountering any face that, just from repetition of seeing, had become familiar.

It is very different here. In one's own neighborhood, one speaks with everyone, and gets to know the children. Nobody feels that he must protect himself against striking up an acquaintance with undesirables. In the course of ordinary errands about town, friendly encounters are common. When one goes to the plaza area, shopping, there is a definite expectation of running into some friend or other.

In New York, it was rare for anyone, friend, acquaintance, or newly met, to say anything about my writing. I felt that, in that great city, those who had read my latest story would be as widely scattered as my personal friends. As a matter of fact, big city people are inhibited. They are afraid of being gushy; they are afraid that if they don't take writing for granted they will seem unsophisticated. Also, scores of writers live in New York; hundreds visit it. In a great city nothing, except perhaps complete openness, is scarce.

Here, if a story of mine comes out, it may be mentioned in the paper. When three or four Santa Fe writers are published in the same month, it is considered news. The little city is frank and warm in its pride. Even more warming to the writer is the habit people have of stopping him in the street to tell him that they have enjoyed his last piece. Strangers will sometimes introduce themselves to do this. It is the kind of thing that makes a writer's life really worth living.

From time to time, people even speak well of this column to me. Give me a small town. Or, to be specific, give me the City Difficult, the home of the broken bottle and the rutted street; give me Santa Fe.

Understanding
the "City Different"

IT'S GOING TO BE a dry year. From Trinidad all the way across to here, the country is browner than I've ever seen it at this season. The grass is dead; the rivers are autumn low. We're in for a nasty, hot, dusty drought.

This will affect people's dispositions deleteriously. All sorts of things are going to happen. The rate of knife fights and shootings from Rio en Medio to Taos is going to double. Burros will become cantankerous, horses will kick, cats will chase dogs.

Twelve miles beyond Abiquiu on a very hot afternoon a frenzied Pueblo Indian will bust an Apache in the snoot, and the Apache will sit down and cry. Whereupon the Apache's wife will light into the Pueblo's wife, and the people at Blanco de Burro will try to break them up and become involved, and eventually someone will send for the state police.

A very good-natured man named Doniciano Rodriquez will causelessly suspect his neighbor of stealing his firewood, and will bore holes in several sticks and fill them with gunpowder. In the heat he will forget to tell his wife. His wife will blow up the stove, sending herself to the hospital. At the time, there will be a pressure cooker on the stove and this, too, will explode, scalding the cat.

Thereafter, Doniciano will call on his wife in the hospital, very penitent, and she will throw her bowl of oatmeal at him. It will bounce off his head and hit Sister Maris Barbara, who will be passing by. All in all, Doniciano will get very much in bad and will never be the same man again. No one will ever know what became of the cat.

A sorrel mule at Bishop's Lodge called Emilio will become exasperated by the established social superiority of the horses, whose mentality he despises, and will lead a revolt of the masses against them. The ensuing kicking and biting contest, which would have been worth a fortune in the movies, will send two wranglers to bed with nervous prostration.

A sweet old children's horse called Buttercup will be so upset by this and by the heat that the next time that horrible little brat, Johnnie Cooper, tries to play Heigh-yo Silver on him, he will reach around and bite the little beast severely in the leg. Johnnie's resulting incapacitation will grieve no one but his mother, and will materially lengthen the life of the wrangler assigned to supervise the little lad.

As the nights will be too hot to sleep, the little boys of Santa Fe will stay up until all hours exploding firecrackers. This will result in the common sight of respectable citizens throwing shoes, hairbrushes, and crockery at shadows. Finally several little boys will injure themselves severely and everyone will be pleased. By then it will be late in August and the citizenry will be well along on the way to going slowly mad. This will result in a number of new and unusual features during Fiesta.

In Tapacitos, a Mr. Axel Surmbrod will be taking a shower at the moment when his wife will decide to water her only remaining patch of flowers. The well being very low, there will be very little water, and the shower will go off when Mrs. Surmbrod turns on the hose, which will be just when Axel has finished soaping himself. Infuriated, he will rush out of the house just as he is, seize the hose, and attempt to beat his wife over the head with the brass nozzle of it.

She will run like mad. He will pursue her, clutching the

hose. Reaching the end of the hose's length, it will snap back on him and he will be catapulted into Efemerio Sandoval's backyard. Efemerio will try to capture what at first he believes to be the pilot of a flying saucer, but Axel will be too slippery for him, and will return home literally in a lather.

Efemerio's description of what he saw will lead to the belief that there is a man loose in the village who has been bitten by a hydrophobia skunk; a general panic will ensue, and state police will be sent for again. The whole place will go slightly haywire.

Axel meantime will have finished his shower and forgiven his wife, who will cook him a dinner of Swedish meatballs. The state cops will go away mad, and that will be that.

Now in the hot weather, with the opera started, July upon us, and visitors pouring in, it is time to offer a few words to help our friends from elsewhere to understand Santa Fe, the City Difficult.

Here in Santa Fe we like to do things the hard way, or at least the roundabout way. For instance, we build an open-air opera at an altitude of approximately seven thousand feet, and it plays during the thunderstorm season. Nonetheless, in characteristic fashion, it puts on more performances than it cancels and everybody has a very good time out there.* The opera people, incidentally, assay considerably higher in personal charm than those you will meet (if you can arrange it) around the Met.

Santa Fe really is the oldest capital city in the United States. That is an authentic fact, even though the Spanish did settle St. Augustine earlier. The Indians you see around town are also genuine. They are not hired to walk the streets or sit under the portal of the Palace of the Governors and look picturesque. They just naturally are picturesque, and you see

* Santa Fe Opera now guarantees performance with a largely covered theater.

them around because they are attending to their business.

The Indians put on dances from time to time in the villages, which are called pueblos (pronounced pwayblos). Almost all of the dances are authentic and are put on by the people who work very hard at them for no pay at all, because they believe in doing them and this is their tradition.

In some villages they will charge you for taking pictures; in some, they will just take your camera away. This saves you money and effort and allows you to look at the dance. If there were no white people at all to come to the dances, spend money, and gawk, the Indians would still be dancing.

You will see green signs on College Street and on the New Lamy Road announcing that there is the Old Santa Fe Trail. It is not. Santa Fe's greatest single asset here being authenticity, many people go in industriously for the phoney. This is an old Santa Fe characteristic.

In fact, there is a powerful element in this town that hates anything authentic. Fifteen years ago, there were near the plaza, in addition to the Palace of the Governors, six old buildings of very interesting character and all of historical value, representing four different periods or influences in local, adobe architecture. Of these two now remain. All the others have been pulled down to provide parking lots. This is definitely a new Santa Fe characteristic. In older times, we just let priceless buildings decay; now we have bulldozers. This is Progress.

It is against the law to sell alcoholic beverages of any kind on Sunday in New Mexico. This law is very highly thought of, as it makes dealing in liquor on Sunday so much more profitable.

As this is being written, a new supertax on cigarettes is going into effect. The tax, it is hoped, will bail out our schools, which have gone broke hiring personnel directors. A group of high school seniors is earnestly trying to improve the level of education in the Santa Fe High School. The school authorities are doing their best to discourage them, which is why the school board just extended the superintendent's contract. This may seem bewildering to an outsider, but here in the City Difficult it is standard operating procedure.

Having mentioned the Indians, I should say a word about the native inhabitants of this city, the Spanish-Americans. They are also authentic, and they are not Mexicans. They fought for this country in the Apache and Navaho Wars, the Civil War (which some would say makes them Yankees), the Spanish War, both World Wars, and in Korea.

Another local tribe is the art colony, but when we come to that, I find myself somewhat involved and probably not objective, so we'll just pass that one up.

In the Odyssey, talking about his distant, native Ithaca, Odysseus says, approximately, "It is a harsh land, but it breeds good young men." Then he adds thoughtfully, "I suppose everyone feels that his own country is the sweetest."

His words apply very well to New Mexico, in fact to the whole Southwest. This is a harsh land. It is an insatiable land. You have three or four days of hard rain, much of which runs off the open range to go rampaging down dry arroyos and on into the Rio Grande; and in a day or two afterwards, the earth is again dry as a bone. Even in our urban, level, well-grassed and tended yards and patios, the moisture is soon gone, and we are back to the hose and more food for faster billing.

When first I came into this country, most people related closely to it. Above all, that was an important part of the charm of Santa Fe. Even the most desk-bound Anglos took pack trips, or went out in the autos of the period, over the dirt roads of the period, into the desert, mountain, and valley country. They were close to it, knew how its people lived, understood the value of a rainstorm, and knew what sand was like to sleep on.

Now here is a news story from Chinle that begins, "A three-day trail ride — the first ever conducted on an Indian reservation — will start from here September 2."

I am astounded to see how far the separation of urban people, in this case, of publicity and newspapermen, from the Southwest has gone. I should not be; it is all around us. Here in Santa Fe today you will encounter people who deplore a few successive days of rain. They find them unpleasant; and, after all, they have city water for their gardens, if they plant at all. Thirty years ago, that would have been impossible.

This seldom applies to the Spanish-Americans. Many of those in Santa Fe have close ties of blood and friendship with the people of the farms, villages, and ranches. All of them seem to keep a sense of the harsh and thirsty land and of the pure beneficence of rain. To an Easterner, raised on "Rain, rain, go to Spain," the true Southwestern delight in wetness was a revelation.

As to that trail ride, three days in the Navaho country: A trail ride is gobbledygook for a pack trip; and, having in my time packed from Santa Fe to the Grand Canyon and ridden the Navaho reservation also from north to south, the statement "first ever conducted" fills me with sadness.

You used to arrange to pack out from Kayenta, where the Wetherills held forth, or from Cosey McSparron's at Chinlee (as we spelled it then), or from the Bishop's Lodge or Los Cerros in Santa Fe. To say "trail ride" was silly, since you never rode anything but trails if you could help it. Some of the trails were mighty dim.

The Bishop's Lodge, when Jack Lambert was head wrangler and dudes were tough and willing, was prepared to carry you horseback clear to the Snake Dances, and do it with comfort. Now the wonderful genus "dude" has just about disappeared.

What we have are motorists, seeking the deluxe motel at the edge of the main, paved route, with Teevee in every room, to spend a single night and move on, seeing America at sixty or seventy miles an hour. It's better than staying home, because of the pleasing sense of motion.

In New Mexico, they see a lot of arid country, pause to walk around the plaza here, to gawk in a pueblo or two, and become reluctant connoisseurs of billboards. The Navaho tribe, more civilized than we, outlawed billboards some years ago. I hope that some of those who take that trail ride will get a real glimpse of this cruel yet endlessly giving land and at least glimpse the meaning of the wonderful gift of occasional water.

We went up to Taos the other day and a very pleasant trip it was in this autumn weather we are having, glorious weather from the point of view of the visitor or the town-dweller, not so good from the point of view of the man with stock to graze on the range. We took the road by Truchas and on through the mountains, which was well worthwhile.

The aspens are gone and the oak brush has turned pretty brown, but I do not ever remember seeing the cottonwoods more beautiful. They varied from a pale gold to a color with orange underlying it, glowing under the sunlight. A few still had spots of green to give a little accent. Minor bushes were an assortment of reddish shades. The fields varied from bare earth through the warm, pale color of stubble all the way to green. The ristras of chile were past the early, scarlet stage, but they still held a clear, deep red and some of the early shiny quality, rather than the matt-surfaced, brownish dragon's-blood they turn to when they are fully dried.

Passing the little farms, we saw corn being brought in, and here and there some had already been shucked and stacked, to add another element to the autumn's red-yellow-brown color scheme. On some portales there were piles of pumpkins, a richness of them; on others, they had begun cutting and drying them. There was the generous feeling over all of the fall of a good year, with lots of hay piled on top of the rustic barns — and what on earth is more absolutely and more genuinely rustic than a New Mexico mountain barn?

Up in the mountains there was still water in the rivers and in many of the ditches, although the rivers were low. It was a good time of year all round for going by that particular route. We all know and travel it from time to time, but in our hurry we pass it up, and while we think we remember it we don't, until something prods us into making the effort again. Then we see as if for the first time, for instance, the roll of the field-checkered, high llanos around Truchas, the bright patterns of the fields at Penasco, or the quality of the Trampas plaza. We catch the bulk of a church or the low mass of simple houses, or perhaps the rise of a bare slope, against a sky the blueness of which we have taken for granted, and see it all over again.

It is more than the first-time seeing, because in addition to the fresh shock of delight, it calls up the memory and the earlier shocks we thought we remembered but really did not. Perception acquires depth in time and thereby becomes all the stronger.

One reason town-dwellers lose track of the blueness of the sky is that most of us do not often see real horizons. We see the high sky against house, or against the mountains, but we miss the sharp attack of the clear blue cut off close at hand by a slope of slightly higher ground. We go home and if our houses are fortunately situated, we look out at sunsets, but through the changing day our eyes are within rooms and as like as not aimed at desks or workbenches.

That road is rough, but not difficult in dry weather such as we are having. We are too much subject to the tyranny of smooth roads. We ourselves would not have taken that route this time if some older friends, visitors from Texas and quite unaccustomed to the mountains, hadn't driven and enjoyed it a few weeks earlier.

Twenty years ago, in rougher, hotter, slower, weaker-tired cars, everyone drove the dirt roads without giving it a second thought. When the main road to Taos was all dirt and wandered across Tesuque Creek twice, people came and went between there and Santa Fe as freely as they do now. Not a hardier breed; the same people. We let ourselves become slaves of our advantages. Good, hard-surfaced roads are one of our many advantages (except when we use them for casual suicide). They make it possible for us to go from here to there rapidly without discomfort, which is always a convenience to have available and often enough a necessity.

Unfortunately, we let this advantage prevent us from taking rough roads we once used freely. We tend to fall into shuttling like so many trolley cars, our travels as narrowly confined as if we rode in that extinct breed. This applies, I think, to many other activities in our lives. Personally, I'm in favor of all the conveniences I can arrange to have, but I am sadly aware that they tend to shackle me.

The Man with the Calabash Pipe had been gardening. I say "had been" tentatively, as it is difficult to say whether, at any given moment, he has left off or is merely pausing. His garden activities consist of two parts work with the trowel, ten parts pausing to recall the exact wording of quotations from relevant sources, such as the Georgics, and eighty-eight parts contemplation or time out to relight, refill, or simply find his pipe.

His pipe was going at the moment and he sat comfortably on the grass, staring at the 1929 Packard sports car that has rested, ever since I can remember, immobile at the end of his driveway under a decrepit shed. Hearing my footsteps, he let out a slight, luxurious puff of smoke, looked towards me, then waved his pipe in broad invitation to the area of scraggly grass at one side of which he reclined.

"When are you going to get a car that runs?" I asked as I sat down.

I expected annoyance; instead, his eye lit up with the pleasure of a real talker who had been handed the lead he wants.

"I shall get a new one when they equip them with proper accessories," he said.

"Such as?"

"A horn attached to the rear bumper, preferably with a device to make a horrible face pop up when the horn is blown, the horn itself being tuned to sound a loud razzberry, for use on characters who honk from behind without any possible justification — as when one is stopped at a stop sign to let contrary traffic go by."

"That would be a help," I said. "Anything else?"

"A prod or goad that could be thrust forward, with a drill on the end — a large, rather dull drill, with which to bore into the gas tanks of persons who double park in front of the post office, on Lincoln Avenue, and at other such points when traffic is heavy. At the same time that the drill began operation, making a fearsome noise and emitting sparks, another device would pop up, to show through the culprit's rear window a sign reading, "Get Going. You Have Been Warned." He chuckled. "That would do a lot towards eliminating congestion in downtown Santa Fe."

I was about to register an objection, but he waved me down.

"Further, I want a device that should either be licensed only to selected, law-abiding drivers, such as I when and if I drive," he looked smug, "or controlled by a simple radar device so that it is operative only when approaching the crest of a hill. This device would consist in essence of a nozzle, a tank of fluid, and a tank of highly compressed air, installed in the left side of the hood or the false bustle with which modern cars come adorned in the name of conspicuousness. Have you a match?"

I handed him one, and he relit his pipe.

"The first tank would contain a compound of fast-drying, durable enamel of an unpleasant yellow color, and skunk extract. When some maniacal goon passed the driver near the top of a hill, the driver would press a button, the tank would spray, and the goon would be clearly and appropriately marked for all to see."

"You have something there," I said, "but wouldn't there be a risk of pranksters shooting the paint at cars coming the other way?"

"No," he said, "it's self-enforcing. If one attempted that, the other car could return the fire. Besides, if the licensing system were used, this law-enforcement weapon would not fall into the hands of the irresponsible."

I swear that the puff of smoke he emitted formed itself into a halo around his uncombed head.

I said, "One other objection, to your second device. Wouldn't there be a danger, if your drill is emitting sparks — as it would — and the double-parker didn't get going in a hurry, that you'd set his tank on fire?"

An expression of beatific pleasure spread over his learned countenance. "Of course there would be, and there's a consummation devoutly to be wished and a new source of roast pig."

Smokeless Cultures

WELL, NOW, Miss Anne Seymour has been eliminated from *Empire*,* as we were told some time ago would happen. As the members of the class know, your correspondent is one of those disagreeable, but surprisingly numerous, people who do not exactly admire *Empire*, but he regrets Miss Seymour's departure, even though only very rarely, after the initial attempt, has he subjected himself to the show.

We hear nowadays about the non-books, of which so many are being published, usually in deluxe size and shape "to lie on the library table." On, or just off, Broadways, we are going through the phase of the non-plays. On Teevee, the great thing nowadays is the non-actor. Poppa Cartwright in *Bonanza* is the classic example, but non-actors is what *Empire* has been studded with, and, with Miss Seymour's departure, will become 100 per cent studded.

The lady, coming from a slightly older dispensation of Thespians, could act. Singularly little imagination has gone into *Empire* scripts, and the presence of an actress in the cast evidently was something that the writers did not know how to handle, or, more likely, that the producer did not let them. Writers for the idiot box live difficult, frustrated lives, with a massive formation of creative incompetents, back to, and including, the sponsor, having the say over every word they put down.

* A TV serial, much of it filmed around Santa Fe.

But Miss Seymour could act. She had stage presence. Charm and personal quality came through, in the poor, lame parts that she was mostly handed. Our kids are likely to grow up under the impression that an actor is any gravel-voiced athlete who can stare into the camera with an intense expression and sock a villain, an actress any cute chick who recites and who possesses three facial expressions and a good scream. Of course Miss Seymour had to go. I should not kick, as I don't give a whoop about the show, but it was nice knowing she was around. Alone of the cast, she was the one that even a blue-nosed frog could feel he would like to meet. I wish her many fat parts in plays and shows of quality.

I don't know when Santa Fe was first used for a film location. The first outfit I remember was King Vidor's, in the early '30's, here to put us on the map, as usual, by making some scrumptious classic. Somehow, the opus has failed to come ringing down the annals of the drama.

The company rather took over La Fonda and was as big about itself as usual, the paper rather less impressed than it has been in the most recent instance, the populace curious but not overwhelmed. It was fun when Louisa Pugh, God bless her and keep her memory green, came into the cantina in her jodhpurs, was introduced to the great and famous benefactors, and informed them and all others assembled there, in well-chosen words and clear, carrying tones, that neither she nor the community of Santa Fe in general were at all impressed by their presence. To steal Wodehouse's eloquent expression, it did them more good than a week at the seaside, and it caused great and general joy.

We were a smaller, more homogeneous settlement then, considerably poorer, and somehow happier and more independent. We related much more closely to our own surrounding, rural community. Our architects were busy elaborating and perfecting the revival and modernization of the Santa Fe style after the initial, eclectic orgy of the art museum. Foreigners up from Albuquerque could not understand why we did not tear down all our mud houses.

Santa Feans as a whole knew what it was they loved in their little city, and that they intended to keep. We had fewer nervous malcontents urging us to transmute our real gold into a debased currency of paper dollars. This writer was one of those who had come to the place out of casual curiosity, skeptical, to spend a fortnight, and been staggered by delightful reality into more visits and then into moving in.

In 1926, an organization of Texas women proposed to establish a "Culture Colony" or Chautauqua settlement near Sunmount, within Santa Fe's city limits. They announced that the colony would bring 3,000 women at a time to the city for visits of many weeks' duration. The Chamber of Commerce went all out to promote the project, and the City Council voted to give the Southwestern Chautauqua a tract of land almost for nothing. At that point the citizens of Santa Fe woke up.

In those days we had an art colony that packed a real wallop. It contained such redoubtable members as Alice Corbin, Mary Austin, and John Sloan. Sinclair Lewis was a visitor. I mention only those no longer with us, lest in citing the living, accidentally I offend by omission. It was around that same time that the art colony routed the D.A.R. when it attempted to stick a "Pioneer Mother" statue in the plaza.

The art colony led the initial attack against the proposed Chautauqua, but it by no means fought unaided. In those days, Santa Fe was small; it was a lively, delightful place, full of fun and creative work, and it knew where it was going. Santa Feans as a whole were then too intelligent to think that growth in itself meant progress, or that an enlarged population made people either happier or more prosperous. Three thousand culture-seekers from Texas, or from anywhere, bringing with them all the banalities of the Chautauqua circuit, were exactly what Santa Fe did not want. The Chamber of Commerce was made to go sit in the corner. The City Council reconsidered its offer. The leaders of the proposed Culture Colony were led to believe that, after all, Santa Fe was not quite the place they were looking for. That was the end of it.

If you had come before the Santa Feans of those days with talk of bringing "smokeless industries" to Santa Fe, you would have been quickly squelched. The people who had settled here had done so, as have so many since, for love of the place — and, being independent thinkers, they knew better than to let the received slogans of Babbittry seduce them into destroying the very thing they loved.

By 1940, our city's population reached 20,000. It had doubled in less than twenty years. The increase had not brought general prosperity, but rather included an increase in the number of the destitute. The place was no better to live in, no more fun, no livelier, no more comfortable, than it had been at 10,000.

Now we have passed 30,000. On the whole, through all these decades, we have been fortunate in the kind and quality of those who have joined us here, but mere growth by numbers has gained us nothing. We are a trifle less comfortable than we were, our city a little less attractive, less distinctive. With numbers comes a definite tendency for us to become more like other American small towns, whereas twenty years ago we tended to increase our difference from them.

Now, as a matter of fact, for some forty years Santa Fe has successfully attracted a group of "smokeless industries," in the form of writers, artists, and just plain bird-watchers. They are impractical, dreamy people who prefer a small intimate town that is as unlike ordinary towns as possible, but they spend highly practical sums of money and are of no small importance to our economy. They look with frank disfavor on economic development committees and similar contrivances. I am one of this little band of loonies, filing herewith what is, I fear, very much of a minority report.

The Man with
the Calabash Pipe: II

"FOR A DOLLAR and a quarter," said the Man with the Calabash Pipe, "we might at least get water."

He poured a rose-colored fluid into his glass from a long-necked, handsome bottle.

"I am referring," he went on in a severe tone, "of course, to the Public Service Company's recent decision. According to that sheet you write for, it is going to cost us all one and one-fourth dollars per month, average. Average, as any Navaho can tell you, is never typical. Just as a mythical, average Navaho draws an income that makes six men in Gallup furious while dozens of Navaho children go without their lunches, so somewhere you will find a customer whose water bill increases only by ten bits."

He knocked off to draw breath (which he needed), and to fill his pipe.

I said, "Well, with their IBM machines —"

He waved me down with a lighted match. "You yourself have said it, only the trouble with you is that, like Mossadegh, you clown at your own trial. They have Faster Billing. Their bills are full of square holes, and must not be spindled, folded, or written upon. Now they also have Larger Billing. Faster and Larger, or Get Thar Fustest with the Mostest, as Gen. Forrest, a highly cultivated Southern Gentleman, never said. Will they also deliver wetter water?"

"It seemed wet to me —" I interpolated.

"Probably, given the habitually numb condition of your senses. That highball (I was pleased by his use of the singular) you had last night — would you call that water?"

Like Mossadegh, in his turn, he answered himself. "No. And if you had had to tell it to a judge, you couldn't have got away with it. So why should this fluid that emanates from our taps at the present moment be denominated water? The Public Service Company has a franchise to deliver water to us, but why should it base its faster bills upon that? The compound it is now serving contains an assortment of minerals that will prevent rickets, stick to the glass, and cause the beard to break off like a stalactite. If Reddy Kilowatt were as fast with his bills as he likes to think he is, he would let the Public Service Company stew in its own juice with a picket fence around it —"

He stopped, put down his pipe, rose, and slowly disentangled himself from his own metaphor while I watched in awe.

"One of my wisest friends," he said, "is a connoisseur of hippopotami. He says that lady hippopotami have more overall appeal then Rita Hayworth, and he has something there. He was planning to donate a hippo to the kids' swimming pool as soon as it was ready, to give the infants something to climb on, but he has given up the idea. Why?"

He leant forward and shook his finger at me. "Why?"

In self-defense I lit a cigarette.

"Because there will be no water in that pool," he said ominously. "Hippopotamusses, in a state of nature, live in the upper waters of the Nile, which derive from the translucent snows of Kilimanjaro (see Hemingway). Now, how would you expect a hippopotamus that is accustomed to bathing in Hemingway's limpid prose, or to being shot at by Hemingway's limpid rifle at fifty cents a word (including 'bang!') to disport itself in this concoction that we are now about to have sold to us by the pound?"

With a sudden gesture of hospitality he poured me a glass of wine.

"It won't work," he said. "If the Chamber of Commerce, the Santa Fe Industrial Development Committee, and the Fiesta Council were on the ball, they would realize that we have now stolen the play away from Ojo Caliente. I don't say that we have arsenic in our water, but I'm sure we could arrange that, and the rings on our bathtubs are getting more and more magnificent. Santa Fe is rapidly ceasing to be picturesque, colorful, or even different — but what a spa it would make!"

I said, rising, "I'm sorry, I have to go write my column. That's hard, and furthermore, I'm in no lather."

"I wish you well," he answered. "By the way, see that wet stuff just outside the door? That comes from melting snow. That, just in case you've forgotten, is water."

On Courts—and the Crossbow

EVEN IN AS very small a town as Santa Fe, the chasm that separates much of the urban population from the ranch life around us is astonishing, an observation prompted by recent letters concerning Bostrom and the penalty for killing a cow. An "archaic" law, they say, makes this offense a felony. Pardon him. Make cattle rustling a misdemeanor.

The critter was killed with an arrow from a crossbow. This somehow makes the act even more commendable. Shoot me with an arrow, stab me with a flint knife, or hit me with an atom bomb; the difference to me would be nil. The same goes for that cow, and for its unfortunate owner, whom nobody mentions.

Let someone break into a workshop and wreck, say, a $250 lathe in order to get some parts he badly needed, and even if he were dressed from head to toe in Lincoln green, no one would consider the offense merely quaint. In this particular case, as this newspaper somewhat belatedly reported, Mr. Bostrom had used his arrows on at least five other cows; the last one was the one he got caught with. Shooting arrows at cows, it seems, can become a vice, like picking your nose, and equally should be prevented.

The comparison of a cow to a lathe is not as far-fetched as it may seem. Both are productive instruments, although the cow's rate of depreciation is higher, its productivity lower. A run-of-the-mine beef cow is at present worth $225–250. For six or seven years it will bear calves which will sell in the fall for $120–140, then culled as superannuated, the animal herself will bring about $115. Even deducting the small amounts needed for pasturage and some feeding, this is an important investment, a valuable article.

The loss, even to a large operator, is serious; to a small one, it could be ruinous.

Details about this particular critter are not handily available. I assume that it was ordinary, a poor man's cow, one might say. At present, a pure-bred three-year-old will bring up to $400, and a pure-bred bull calf raised to bullhood can bring anywhere from $300 to $2,000, not counting blue ribbon show animals.

Anyway you fry it (or broil it), taking a cow is no small theft. Under the law as we conceive it, it makes no difference whether the owner is rich or poor; the offense is the same. Two to ten years, in this state, usually means two years if the convict behaves at all well. That is not so heavy a punishment.

The history of the modern West proves that, with cattle temptingly scattered over open range, rustling is a practice that quickly revives wherever circumstances are favorable. A lazy sheriff, for instance, or fair assurance that the rustler will get off light.

The practice comes in two principal flavors — killing for meat by impoverished neighbors, and carting stock off in trucks for sale. The latter practice at times, when rings have been discovered, has run into hundreds of heads. The former is an involuntary form of direct charity that is not usually considered a usual mode of rehabilitation for unfortunate people. As a device for survival in the woods, I don't think most of us would want to see boy scouts instructed in it.

If, however, we are to have a new deal under which all

freedom-loving cattle rustlers are pardoned provided they use
arrows, or the law is to be rewritten to make this practice a
misdemeanor (how about horses? dogs? boy scouts?), then
there should be a parallel rule or law condoning the theft of
small, valuable objects, provided the taker wears a green cap
with a feather in it. Only I want this law written or this custom established so that it does not condone the taking of any
animals or articles of mine. This is the kind of law one
wants strictly for other people.

This newspaper covered rather fully the hearings of the
State Judicial System Study Committee, of which Senator Fa-
bian Chavez is chairman, in its investigation of the Justice of
the Peace System. Now the committee's findings have been
published, under the title of "The Courts in New Mexico."
This is a booklet that every citizen should read, with pleasure and dismay — pleasure at the brisk, effective, clear, and
lively presentation, dismay at the facts.

The volume runs to 49 plus v pages; it is printed by the
Rydal Press, and I understand that you can get it for free if you
ask the New Mexico Legislative Council for it politely. Only
once before have I reviewed a free book, and that one, a
checkbook, contained much fewer words than does this, but
this little number really deserves to be called to the public's
attention.

The committee was able to get the JP's to talk very frankly.
It also got remarkable material out of the state police and various district attorneys and judges. Packed well together, the
resultant information is highly quotable.

We may begin, just as a sample of the wonderful stuff the
JP's themselves furnished, with the remark that "a justice of
the peace should maintain a great deal of levity and dignity"
in his court, by the same JP who held that a justice "shouldn't
be a habituary of bars, that he shouldn't hold court in un-

dignified surroundings, such as in a saloon or in a gas station."

But another man testified: "I received over 100 cases that I tried in a cafe booth." Another held court in a chicken house, and a third sometimes heard — and presumably still hears — cases in a coal mine he operates. Such settings, and characters such as the one who held court with nothing on above the waist, the many gents who state that they always find traffic or other offenders guilty, and the one who ensures a guilty plea from out-of-state defendants by setting the date of trial five days off, form the image of New Mexico justice, as the report notes, that many visitors encounter.

The report says, "The JP's, thus, are as well equipped to handle legal matters as lawyers would be to do carpentry work, especially if the lawyers refused to acquire any other tools than a tack hammer and perhaps a saw. Yet the public, which would never consider hiring lawyers to do carpentry work, apparently acquiesces in carpenters acting as judges."

Then there is the JP who, near the end of the year, asked the police to stop enforcing the law as all his take would be going into income tax. And another who said, "All the cases we handle are just simple: rape attempt, rape, breaking and entering, beating up a man . . . robbery, armed robbery," and the one who found that a man shot three times through the heart and once through the head had committed suicide.

The system, the report shows, tends to corrupt our police, state and local. At another point, it says, "There is no single point at which the administration of the justice of the peace system is especially weak. The JP courts are administered in an especially weak manner at all points."

That, friends, is style, and so is the remark "There is no intention here of supplying a manual as to how to embezzle money from the state of New Mexico. Only practices completely known throughout the entire JP system will be mentioned." You really should read what follows; it is fascinating. Another nice bit of writing is, "Until recently, few JP's bothered with tampering with receipts. The reason is comparatively simple: many JP's often did not issue receipts at all."

The Man with
the Calabash Pipe: III

"I SEE," said the Man with the Calabash Pipe severely, "that you've taken out after the bills sent out by the largest and most necessary firms in town." He paused to relight his pipe.

I seized upon the opening. "Yes, especially the Public Service. Their latest bill traces my account all the way back to May, heaven knows why. I had to read for half an hour to find out —"

He cut me short with a wave of his freshly fuming pipe. "Essentially petty, irrational, and possibly subversive. Big business is defending us all in the battle of man against the machine. For instance, have you ever subscribed to *Time*? Have you ever received a renewal notice from that publication?"

I said, "I have," and he frowned slightly at the interruption.

"You may have noticed that, no matter how promptly you renew, you will continue to receive ever more dramatic follow-up solicitations. Don't interrupt. They all come breathlessly, with air-mail collect return envelopes. A person like yourself would doubtless succumb to the temptation to mail back the empty envelopes and let the magazine pay up. I, on the other hand, corresponded with them. I got as high as the fourth assistant manager of the circulation department."

He sucked furiously at his pipe a moment to renew its fire. I did not say anything because I have, in fact, been guilty of putting collect return envelopes, or whatever you call them, empty in the mail when the solicitation annoyed me.

"The fourth assistant manager," he said from behind a fresh cloud of smoke, "told me that owing to the efficiency of *Time*'s machine records and machine solicitation devices, it took four weeks from the day on which a subscription is received before the automatic mailing of follow-ups can be stopped. In the interval, the renewal is being 'processed,' a word which means that the user is too lazy to say what he means.

"The interesting thing was that the fourth assistant stated this fact proudly. What people like you fail to see is that these firms are busy defeating the machines. They have elaborated their automatic devices to a point of charming confusion. Far from putting people out of jobs, they have created thousands of new jobs, but of a much pleasanter sort. For myself, I'd far rather supervise a machine, comfortably aware that most of what it is doing is absolutely superfluous, than sit and type out bills or notices that are actually due."

He shifted slightly in his armchair. "What you lacked the honesty to admit in your column is that, in fact, you dislike all bills. So do I."

Leaning back, he let a trickle of smoke escape from between his lips while he looked at the ceiling beatifically. "In a perfect world, one would charge everything and no one would ever send bills. That would be the millennium. Unhappily, it shows no sign of arriving. All one can do is classify bills as to their objectionableness."

He straightened up and continued, marking his points with motions of his pipe stem.

"One may classify bills according to amounts, on the absolute and irrefutable basis of the smaller, the less distasteful. Unfortunately, it is a classification that alters from month to month. The least objectionable bills are those with which a return envelope is enclosed. It's an appreciable courtesy, and should receive recognition.

"There is the general run of simple bills, about which one can say little except that here they are. Then there is that objectionable class of bills on which the senders stamp PAST DUE if one has let them go for a month. That is a disagreeable and stupid habit. Everyone from time to time lets a bill go for a month. Even the utilities and telephone companies are quite nice about it, and the gas company is the only one that makes a profit from your delay."

He struck another match. "I always put those 'PAST DUE' bills at the bottom of the pile."

He wrapped himself in a fresh and somehow complacent cloud of smoke. I sat bemused. For once, I had found something on which I completely agreed with the Man with the Calabash Pipe.

"One of the most depressing phenomena of the new Age of Inconvenience into which our so-called civilization has drifted," said the Man as he reached for the humidor and fuelled up, "is, not only the outrageous manner in which those who wish to exploit them treat the great mass of sap citizens, as your colleague Harrison so aptly calls them, but the incredible meekness with which the citizens submit to abuse. Have you a match?"

I passed him two, and waited while he lit up.

"I think," he went on, "of my great uncle Ezekiel Witherspoon. Suppose he received one of those astounding solicitations for a contribution to a worthy cause, or for a subscription to a magazine, that say, in part, 'Your name has been obtained from a list that it has not been possible for us to check with our own, so if you have already sent us a contribution (or subscribed to our wretched publication), please excuse this communication,' or rot to that effect."

He puffed hard to bring his pipe back to life.

"I can just see him throwing the appeal or whatever you call it in the wastebasket, cancelling his subscription to the magazine, crossing the charity off his list. I can hear him announcing — quite correctly — that 'not possible to check' meant, in fact, that the outfit was too stingy, too greedy, too slovenly, or all three of these, to take the trouble to avoid a needless discourtesy and cause of annoyance."

He dug in his waistcoat pocket, produced several matches of his own, and lit up again.

"In his day," he said, "no one ever was guilty of such an imposition. Recently, I got a bill from a supposedly reputable, even rather old-fashioned firm that does a sizeable mail-order business, that had printed on it, 'We do not expect you to pay for any goods that have not been received.' How quickly Great Uncle Ezekiel would have severed relations with that firm!"

He took time out to blow several rings. "If you buy something on the installment plan, or have a mortgage at the bank, what happens? You are given a wretched little booklet neatly calculated to fit nowhere and to get lost on your desk. This, it will say, is for your convenience. Convenience! They mean, to save themselves the trouble and slight expense of billing you. A serial number and the amount to be paid each month are marked clearly enough, but can they also put in your name and address? No. You bill yourself, fill in your own name, send off the payment and the slip, and pray that you will remember the miserable device come next month."

His voice had risen. Now he lowered it. "In our modern age of anti-service, your creditors gull you into doing their work for them. It would be a great service to mankind if someone with the money to spare would bill one of these corporations for his services and fight it through. If nothing else, it would be great fun to watch."

Producing a special tool for the purpose he had been given for Christmas, he tamped his tobacco.

"It all fits in with 'faster billing' — which our friends the Public Service Company advertised as a convenience — with 'rotary billing,' and with telephone dial systems that can send a simple long distance call 1,000 miles off course. And we all stand for it. This is a degenerate age, rugged individualism is all but dead; thanks to the wonders of modern science, the granite foundations of democracy are being made over into synthetic grey flannel suits."

He puffed at his pipe and relaxed, contemplating his last metaphor with a mixture of surprise and pleasure.

The Bird-Watchers' Wars

MAN BITES DOG department (and no rabies): Various officials of the big Humble Oil Company were in town this week, consulting with local bird-watchers of standing on how to build a service station in Santa Fe that would really fit in with the character of the town. Partly genuine feeling on the part of some of them for the quality of this place, part, no doubt, enlightened self-interest. Would there were more of it!

But it is scarce, and that is why Councilman Leo Murphy's idea of a real control, not merely use-zoning, but preservation of antiquities and architectural supervision of new buildings, so greatly deserves support. It is good to know, too, that Allen Stamm, whom the bird-watchers recently pecked so hard, favors a requirement of real Santa Fe style in at least the design of what goes up.

We seem bent on suicide. It is amazing how many people in this community prefer a fast buck or two to an assured future. We chip and chip away at our great asset, until even the casual visitor begins to notice that things aren't what they are advertised to be. A recent visitor, who had been here some years ago, spoke to me in strong terms of distress at what had happened to the center of town and the swamping of the plaza. Anybody who thinks that thousands and thousands of people are going to keep on coming here just to look at the Governors' Palace, old San Miguel Church, and Cristo Rey, should have his head examined.

When I first came to Santa Fe, I came with deep suspicion. I had lived in Mexico and Central America, and I did not believe anything really Spanish, or Latin-American, could exist in the United States. I expected a Californian fraud. How well I remember coming past where the armory is now and seeing the first of Santa Fe, and the effect of the entrance itself, the irregularity and the authentic character of the first blocks of College Street! I was converted then and there. There is no substitute for the real thing, nothing so effective.

Now some goons are talking of widening College Street — an undertaking that would be as wildly expensive as it would be pointless. The entrance to Santa Fe from the west is a disillusioning shocker that costs us many an overnight visitor. It was inevitable in our slap-happy way of growing; an unzoned, arterial road had to go the way this one has.

We have our by-pass system now. The heavy trucks are routed away from the center of town. The greater part of College Street traffic is passenger cars; to the visitor from the East, it is just the reverse of Cerrillos' ribbon development. It is an uncontrovertible assertion that you are entering a natural, unfaked, ancient settlement of Spanish tradition. It is a street of character until you get down to the lower end of it, where it has been let go to pieces. I understand that there will be a big office building in that vacant lot that will require far more cars than it will provide parking space for. Ah well, the City Difficult.

So the bird-brains (as distinct from the bird-watchers) say, let us build a modern, real Texan, wide street coming in here, so that people can hurry to the heart of town and pile up there at the angle of Water Street and the Shelby Street turn. I can imagine the cars stacked up past Loretto back well beyond the bridge, waiting and honking. Or do they think they can get to tear down the end of La Fonda? Talk of bird-watchers, this one is for the birds.

The more I watch what goes on here, the more I see of life, the more deeply convinced I am that there is nothing more dangerous than the well-intentioned, so-called "practical" man with neither intelligence nor imagination.

The foregoing remarks brought me a most gratifying response, in people who spoke to me, called me up, or wrote letters, some of them entire strangers to me. That kind of thing is most heartening to a writer, but I do urge all those good people that they make their responses where they will really do good, by writing to this newspaper. There are far more of us bird-watchers than we realize, we should make ourselves heard. Our motto should be, "Bird-Watchers of Santa Fe, Unite! You have nothing to lose but your pains!"

The very first communication I had, however, was a dissenting opinion, from a Texas lady with a pleasant voice who took exception to my reference to Texas in the column. She called up at 8:35 A.M. I hold it is not Christian to telephone anyone at 8:35 A.M. on Sunday. I tried to explain to the lady that I had eggs cooking and could not talk to her at that time, but she was in a high dudgeon (estimated at 9,375 feet with the barometer at 28.2) and went right on, so I was forced to hang up on her to save the eggs. I was sorry to do this, and apologize.

She wanted to know why people hereabouts are always taking pokes at Texas. That's a big question, and a full answer would involve about 120 years of history, from the Texas-Santa Fe Expedition down to Texas suing us because we hadn't had enough rain, along with a number of involved cultural observations.

As a matter of fact, I didn't take a poke at Texas. I just said that a four-lane entrance into Santa Fe from the east would be Texas style. It would be. I could have called it Iowa style, or California style, but I used Texas because mention of that state, or republic, arouses a special antipathy — which brings us right back to the lady's question.

Tackle any Santa Fean about Texas and you will get, first, a hostile reaction, second, an admission of friendship with a number of individual Tejanos. Some of my best friends are Texans. We think about Texans, in the aggregate, through a stereotype, a folk-image. That's fair enough, since Texans think about us, and particularly about the Spanish members of our group, also in stereotypes. Our fixed image of Texans is emotionally colored by a mixture of irritation, envy, the memory of past offenses, and a sense of helplessness. After all, there is nothing you can do about a Texan.

Texas is booming, bustling, progressive, standardized, prosperous, enormous, and it exports Texans on a fantastic scale. Most Texans, in our experience, are inordinately proud of being Texans and let you know about it early and often. With a little help from Britain, Brazil, and Brooklyn (another well-advertised principality), they have won several world wars. They have certain racial prejudices that run counter to what Santa Fe stands for. (One Texan, and a charming person, informed me that anyone who has Indian blood is a Mexican. That makes me a Mexican. I have heard of Latins from Manhattan, but a Rhode Island Mexican strikes me as an intriguing novelty.)

These things, and the fact that Texans appear to be somewhat the wave of the future while we have the look of an undertow of the past, get our backs up. And while we are at it, let's admit that Texans buy our books and paintings, and that there are lots of Texans settled here among us who are so delightful, and have fit themselves so well to the Santa Fe scene, that we don't realize they are Texans. Some of the most cultivated, delightful, and thoroughly American people I know are natives of the Lone Star State.

Nonetheless, dear lady, it remains that a four-lane highway entrance into a small town is something that, not without admiration, we expect in mighty Texas, but that would ill become poor, dear, ornery, Santa Fe.

With a good deal of pride and a degree of historical accuracy unusual for these parts we speak of Canyon Road as being the oldest thoroughfare in America. As it has developed in recent years, the authorities have given it a special recognition denied the plaza, a zoning intelligently designed to preserve it as an important part of that old town which, if we don't destroy it entirely, will prove an ever greater economic asset to the city of Santa Fe.

Yet, the city fathers seem absolutely unable to leave the poor old street alone. There are times when I think we were better off under that mayor who explained that it was impossible to do anything about the ruts and chuck holes because the street was so old that the dirt was worn out.

In recent years it has been torn up, excavated, blown up, until at times one feared that there would never be a road there again. It has been paved, thus emphasizing the inconvenience of its narrowness, trebling its danger to driver and pedestrian alike, lessening its antique charm, and in the right kind of weather turning the whole thing into a sluice. Some of this paving or hard coating was not, shall we say gently, done quite as well as it might have been, and failed to stand up. For a brief and welcome period, a lavish distribution of pot holes served to keep traffic strictly under control in several sections.

More recently, in a wet period of spring, and in a state of absent-mindedness or something, the city sloshed a light oil coat over a long stretch of it, scattered sand over that, and went away chuckling. Sure enough, the stuff splashed all over everything, and on that narrow pathway covered not only parked cars and passing people but walls, doors, and windows. It was a mess, and undoing it cost the city a pretty penny.

Well, now, the authorities are planning to do the street over new from the bottom up. The businesses along the road are among those that return the greatest cash benefits to Santa Fe, but on the whole they are maintained by artists, or deal in arts and crafts and writing and such, and rule one for all hard-headed businessmen is never listen to an artist, no matter how much kale he rakes in for the community.

Rule two is kick him in the teeth if you can, and rule three is roll over and play dead for big business from out of town, even if they are engaged in siphoning off the community's money for the benefit of owners in Kalamazoo.

So, the protests of the active business people and residents along Canyon Road produce a glassy-eyed inattention. The plan is, first, to have the Public Service and Gas Companies dig up their old pipes and mains and do all the new laying they need to. We are promised that this will take only a short while, but even those with short memories will remember that the last affair of this kind went on for months and months and the blasting used to throw sick people out of bed.

Then there will be all new paving, a storm sewer, and a sidewalk all along the north side. How in the name of heaven you are going to fit a sidewalk serviceable to anybody but a tightrope dancer into a roadway that even now is in large part too narrow to permit cars to pass each other, nobody has explained. For purposes of rapid transit, Canyon Road is a mess now, but its function is not rapid transit. As a tourist trap, which is its function, it is operating beautifully. Why not leave it alone?

Canyon Road is neither Modrun nor Prahgressive, and, you gentlemen with the passion for improving everything even if it means destroying it, its value lies in its lack of those charac-

teristics. Furthermore, your proposed "improvements" won't
make it Modrun or Prahgressive. It just never will look like
Park Avenue, New York.

If our unstoppable builders and changers want to improve
this unique and richly profitable asset, let them put what
brains they have to creating a new thoroughfare leading to
upper Canyon Road, east of Cristo Rey. The lower road is
the most inadequate thoroughfare in America, old or new,
and the common interest demands that it be relieved of that
burden. This, of course, would take some serious thinking,
even some imagination. But think of all the construction and
pipelaying and the rest that would result from the creating of a
new, Up-To-Date, throughway all the way from the Castillo
Street Bridge to Cristo Rey! The only trouble with the proposal is that it would not inconvenience anybody, and that
would spoil the fun.

Growth of a City:
An American Story

A WHILE BACK, when the question of a new federal building was first discussed, the idea of putting it on, or adjacent to, the present Federal Place caused howls of protest over the possible loss of one of our very few parks and the inevitable worsening of an already bad traffic congestion. Now Mayor Murphy proposes that the new building be located out at the old Pen, and another set of howls rises up, this time from our centrally-located merchants who, on occasion, are just as emotional as the artists and their bird-watching allies.

The fact is that both the merchants (professional and business men) who occupy the traditional, commercial center of the city, and the city as a whole, are in a predicament which is going to grow worse and more unpleasant to resolve the longer we refuse to face up to it. Also, rational discussion of the merits of the various proposed locations for federal offices has been badly confused by the cry that using the Pen site would create an "old town" and a "new town." This is a slogan that arouses a great deal of horror combined with a minimum of thought.

So, to start with, let's look at this dreadful business of an old and new town. There is Old Las Vegas, irrationally and defeatingly a separate municipality from New Las Vegas, and it is in bad shape. For that matter, all of Las Vegas is in pretty poor shape. It does not attract industry, and although it lies on a main transcontinental route, it is unable to build up a serious tourist business. What assets the old town may possess have never been exploited, hardly touched. There is no resemblance between that situation and what we might have here.

Albuquerque has an old town, part of the city, and not too far from the new town business area. Because a new town developed, the old town was saved from ruination. In the last fifteen years or so, with a commendable mixture of aesthetic feeling, historical sentiment, and long-sighted self-interest, what there is of old town, which is mostly the plaza, has been fully and excellently developed.

As a result, Albuquerque has a plaza considerably more attractive than Santa Fe's, Palace of the Governors and all. That plaza is surrounded by businesses suitable to a center for tourists and for local people who care for the old, the picturesque, the artistic, and good enchiladas. It is a real asset to the city. Twenty-five years ago, there was nothing in Albuquerque to cause a tourist to linger even long enough to take a snapshot; today there is a high-class, profitable tourist attraction.

Had not that so-horribly-dreaded phenomenon of old and new towns developed in the Duke City, the little plaza would long since have been spoiled beyond redemption, which is what is likely to happen to our plaza.

In order to give some rational consideration to choices that may save or destroy the heart of Santa Fe, let us begin by disabusing our minds of the idea that an "old town" and a "new town," handy to each other, are necessarily harmful. There are examples beyond New Mexico, such as the old Beacon Hill district of Boston, now subject to such careful restrictions, but the case of Albuquerque should suffice.

Also, for the sake of intelligent argument, let us get it well set in our heads that the question of whether the mayor owns businesses in the vicinity of the site he proposes has absolutely no bearing at all on the desirability of the site. This is an intensely personal and rather suspicious city, and already I have met people whose thought processes on this subject have been chloroformed by that question.

It remains true that if a "new town" develops away from the plaza — which is already beginning to happen anyway — in the course of time a number of merchants now doing business at the old, old stand will have to move. In many cases this will mean great expense; in some cases it could be ruinous. The direct investment of the merchants themselves, most especially of our independent, local merchants, in their buildings is heavy. Naturally they don't want to be forced out.

But there is a great deal more to that situation than the merchants, or the general public, seem to have realized.

The merchants who are objecting so strenuously to the possible development of a new commercial center — a "new town" — near the site of the old Pen, should a new federal building be placed there, are understandably alarmed at the prospective loss of their heavy investment in the properties they now occupy in the traditional commercial center of Santa Fe, on and near the plaza.

Everybody else who has a stake in plaza real estate must be worried, too.

Sunday before last's story on the merchant's vote did not give figures, nor did it tell who voted. I'd like to know more about that. There are a number of merchants in the area, dealers in the things that visitors buy, restaurateurs, and so forth, who would gain immeasurably if the plaza ceased to be a humming, congested commercial center.

All concerned, as a matter of fact, face a serious, long-range threat. The old business district is incapable of handling even the traffic now upon it. Uncontrolled development has made our plaza minimal as a tourist attraction. The whole district

is steadily moving towards becoming a blighted area, and ending up a commercial slum adorned by a few antiquities.
Within a block of the plaza, after a brave start at its intersec-
tion with College, Water Street deteriorates rapidly as you go
west. Beyond Sandoval it is close to a blighted area right
now.

In the rush hours, the traffic in the district, and on the ar-
teries (perhaps some of them would better be called capil-
laries) leading to and from it is already infuriatingly congested. At times it snarls up completely. It is getting to be
unpleasant as a place to go to and shop.

A number of merchants have already seen the writing on
the wall. First of these are those mass-businesses, the super-
markets. Kaune's has abandoned the plaza proper; it and
what is now Barber's have branches outside the district,
while the largest new market, now Piggly-Wiggly, is out on
Cordova Road. It is my observation that housewives would
rather drive a mile to the Cordova Road center than half a
mile downtown.

The banks and a number of businesses have followed the
grocery stores. There are branches and there are main es-
tablishments at each of the new sites. All these are signs.

The central district is a messy mixture today. Part of the
plaza and adjacent parts are truly historic and fascinating.
Part of the new construction consists of fine examples of modern Santa Fe style. Part is nothing at all, and away from the
plaza itself you can expect anything dull. There are businesses aimed at tourists, visitors, and luxury buyers. There
are mass businesses aimed at local residents. There are assorted other businesses. Each type tends to drive the others
out, and that which sells the most for least to the most people tends to win out.

The crowding, the shop windows, the unfortunate structures, turn what should be the best of all our attractions into a disappointment that, literally, causes a certain number of tourists to decide to leave town. So the ancient heart of the city fails in its prime function.

As a main shopping center, a district such as this, inconvenient, badly served by inadequate streets, much of it ratty, is bound to go on deteriorating. Then in the long run, merchants, real estate dealers, property owners will be stuck with depreciated property and the necessity of moving out and selling at a heavy loss. The more concentration we create there, the more we hasten this process.

If, on the other hand, we boldly accept the need for a "new town" mercantile district, if, perhaps, we have the courage to make the plaza itself a pedestrian zone, the values should remain high and those who can deal more profitably in the new town will be able to sell well to those whose greatest profit is to be made in a section that is a natural trap for tourists and for bird-watchers of all kinds.

We are facing something in the nature of a slow disaster. With foresight and courage we can turn it into opportunity, with timidity and lack of thought, we can just sit and let it hit us.

The Man with
the Calabash Pipe: IV

WALKING TO TOWN, I ran into my friend The Man with the Calabash Pipe, roaming along in his usual state of dégagé literary inelegance. Under and behind his pipe he sported a curious beard, a sort of wispy fog of rather curly, black hair marked with grey.

"What on earth," I asked, "are you doing with that thing on your chin?"

"Lending myself an air of solidity and dignity," he said, "since I am going into business."

"Business?"

"Yes, business." He struck a match on the seat of his pants, which were worn thin in a long diagonal from that practice, and puffed at his pipe. "The Burpee Bulldozer Basement & Burial Co. Don't interrupt; I can read your mind. Burpee because the name is irresistible, and sticks in the customer's mind. As for the rest, I have conceived an enterprise geared to the present age, the age of holocausts and excavations."

He blew out a cloud of smoke, waved a well-formed and fairly clean hand, and went on. "We dig basements, bomb shelters, bulwarks, or whatever else you want. As to burials, we intend to fit the undertaking business to modern times, taking it out of small business into big business. Undertakers ——"

"Morticians," I said, determined to get a word in.

He sent a cloud of strong tobacco around my head. "A ridiculous term. This age of realities has no room for euphemisms. Besides, the word's misleading. If it derives from 'mors' it means 'dealer in death'; if from 'mortuus,' then it means 'dealer in corpses.' Actually an undertaker undertakes to take you under; his mission is to remove the unpleasant evidences of mortality and dispose of them in a manner calculated to allow us to continue to show respect without laceration of the feelings."

I always did like his flow of language, it had somewhat the same stupefying effect as the tobacco he smoked, but operated more pleasantly.

"Your philosophy may be sound," I said, "but about the business?"

"Wholesale Rates for Holocausts — Economy Packages for Family Disasters — All the Loved Ones Together. If we can get a State Department license, we shall make contracts with the Iron Curtain countries. Business there must be wonderful. You don't know where one can get a good, used bulldozer on time payments, do you?"

"No, and anyway, that beard. You're too old for that. Get rid of it."

"Too old?" He was shocked. "Are you illiterate? Beards are the emblem of maturity and wisdom."

"Not around Santa Fe they aren't. By accepted convention among the artists and their friends, beards are the symbol of adolescence prolonged beyond voting age. I admit you're peculiar" (he smirked faintly) "but in your own curious way you've grown up. Take it off."

"It does tickle," he said, pulling uncertainly at the fringe, "but still — so much trouble to raise." Then he brightened. "Anyway, if I can't get a bulldozer I can't go into business, so I shan't need it. Have you seen my new pamphlet, 'The

54 Around and About a City

Cause and Cure of Wives'? I think it's going to be a sell-out."

"Maybe that beard becomes you after all," I said thoughtfully.

He looked at me with suspicion, puffed vainly at his pipe, knocked out the ash, refilled it lavishly, and lit up, surrounding himself with odorous fog. Suddenly he stepped back into open air with a cry. "It's caught fire!" He clapped his hand to his chin.

He turned and ran towards Santa Fe River, his hat flapping, his pipe waving in his right hand. I went on back home, to try to figure what on earth to put in this week's column.

Santa Fe vs. Santa Fe

THERE IS A VERY, very elegant and intelligent magazine called *Horizon*, which is considerably too expensive for the likes of me. I see it now and again in other people's houses or through the kindness of a friend.

Its September number runs a highly favorable article on an architect named Louis Kahn. The article contains a sentence that is well worth pondering: "But Kahn has arrived on the scene at a time when architecture is hungry for daring new departures."

Viewing history, we can see that even in ancient times architecture underwent continuous change. We can see also that not all of these changes were fortunate. Even so, the mind boggles at trying to imagine what it would be like if style and design had been frozen for all time at, let us say, even the very peak of Greek or Roman times.

Architecture changes in response to several influences. One is the discovery or invention of new engineering techniques and new materials. The discovery of the arch and invention of concrete, for instance, were bound to cause revolutions. Then, throughout time there has been a constant process of change in the function of buildings, in what the users wanted them for. Even in simple residences today's rich man wants something very different from what a twelfth century baron required before he could feel secure.

There is also, thank goodness, the restless, esthetic man,

particularly the architects themselves. In a free society, like
any artists, they are bound to be inspired to improve and in-
novate. Of course, not all architects are artists, any more than
all artists are; and in any field of art, nothing is more deadly
than the innovations of the incompetent seeking to be striking.

Materials, techniques, and needs are changing ever more
rapidly, and it is inevitable that the pace of architectural
change should be stepped up accordingly. The danger in this
— and I read it in the quotation above — is the idea of
change for change's sake, of style and "daring new departures" cooked up much as women's clothes designers and
hairdressers cook up new styles for the fair sex.

Last year's hairdo simply disappears along with last year's
shade of lipstick. Last year's dresses, if they cannot be altered,
can be stored or destroyed, as can the paintings that responded to last year's fad. Sculpture is more difficult, but
consider the tens of thousands of cast-iron animals and vapid
Psyches that have somehow disappeared from the scene. As
to last year's writing, it is easily done away with.

Last year's architecture is something else. It is inclined to
stick around. Yes, buildings are razed, but not according to
their beauty; rather, according to blind economic chance that
often destroys the best and leaves the most hideous. It will be
a long time before we recover from the recent orgy of almost
solid glass walls, monotonous to the eye and functionally in-
defensible, that have been such a boon to the venetian blind
and air conditioning manufacturers.

So when we are offered a novelty, we should think it over
with some care, as when making up our minds to marry (but
how often we don't think that over; see Ann Landers). The
more important the building, especially the more sure we are
that it will have to last a really long time, the more carefully

we should think it over. A layman who doesn't listen to the advice of architects is asking for trouble; but remember, also, that architects, in the joy of what one might call sculptural inspiration, also sometimes forget the human beings who must inhabit, or work in, and in any case, gaze upon the structure they have conceived, year after year.

All of which adds up to a hope that we may all have a chance to see, study, and digest the proposed design for additions to the state capitol. It sounds exciting and could become the pride of New Mexico, but once it's up, it's up. I hope we can look it over first, with our minds neither made up that we must have novelty nor that we must repeat the familiar.

The Old Santa Fe Association is having a mighty try at saving Santa Fe from itself, and every good citizen should rally around, with his clearly expressed support and his dollars.

Tearing down the Nusbaum Building to provide a parking lot is one of those easy ways out that even the best intentioned of city administrations sometimes fall for. We must not let it happen.

In the center of town we have a varied assortment of buildings in the modern adaptations of the Santa Fe style, some very good, some medium, some bad. We have a number of unamiable leftovers. And we have a very few structures that act as the guarantee of the reality of Santa Fe, the old, unselfconscious buildings that just naturally grew in their native style, unpretentious, priceless, and vitally important. Of these, the Nusbaum house is one.

If parking space were the only consideration, the practical thing to do would be to tear down that old Governors' Palace, move the museums to Pecos Road, and get your parking lot where it would be the very most accessible.

Such a suggestion sounds absurd — but consider. The Pal-

ace once stood in a context of authentic, old buildings, in
which it was the key feature. Most of these have been destroyed. Between it and the Prince Patio and Sena Plaza
stands a filling station. Elsewhere near the plaza there is
nothing of the old and natural but the Nusbaum house. On
Washington Avenue you have the filling station, the Torreon
group, certainly no architectural gems, then the unfortunate
Greer Building. Beyond that, for the moment, still stands the
Nusbaum Building, with its powerful authenticity, its real
uniqueness, its great charm.

Pull it out and put in that parking lot, then stand by the
Public Library, and what will you see? An unbroken series
of parking lots running all the way back across Otero Street
to Radio Plaza. South of this fine Olde Spanysshe display of
parked cars will be the drab, non-conforming north wall of
the Greer Building, as colorful as a small factory, then the
outbuildings and rear ends of the Prince aggregation, which
have not been kept up as their fronts have. In short, right
around the corner from the plaza itself, within view from the
Palace of the Governors, we should have a major eyesore.
The harm to Santa Fe would be incalculable.

A few years ago the Santa Fe Railway tore down three of
the few remaining old buildings in the center of town, the
Lamy-Whelan complex on Cathedral Place, which included
two real museum pieces, to put in a parking lot. Suddenly
Santa Fe lost incalculable values in grace, authenticity, and
appeal.

There seems to be a magic about parking lots and service
stations. The city fathers permit them in the most sensitive
areas, without any apparent consideration of the damage they
do.

Now, the Old Santa Fe Association has come up with a
sensible and practical plan that will take the city off the finan-

cial hook on which it has hung itself on the quiet, provide a good bit of parking, and save the old building and its trees. The cost, according to preliminary studies, should be a good deal less than pessimistic members of the city council figured. Nonetheless, it will cost money.

So here is where Santa Feans can stand up and be counted. Somewhere around $25,000 must be raised. Perhaps we can get some of it from outside. Most of it we ourselves must produce.

Further report: the struggle to save, or against saving, the Nusbaum house has brought out a number of factors that should be carefully considered by all concerned, including the members of the city council.

The Old Santa Fe Association held what amounts to the most difficult and unlikely referendum possible in that the votes cast in favor of saving the building were in the form of cash payments and firm pledges. (Hereabouts, voters more commonly expect to be paid to vote.) The returns were nonetheless much larger than anticipated, both in terms of the amount raised and the numbers of those contributing.

Among the contributors were a great many people of limited means, plain, ordinary citizens, who sent in what they could, often with covering notes expressing their deep concern over the proposed razing. The Chamber of Commerce should also note that a number of contributions came from outside the state, from people who visit, know, and care for Santa Fe. This is strong evidence that the building as it stands is a needed asset to the city.

Those who want the house pulled down fall into two principal groups. One consists of people who simply don't see why a somewhat dilapidated, shabby, abandoned building should not be got rid of. They are not, it would seem, impressed by an age of a hundred years. Of course, if people don't think that a certain style is attractive, you can't argue it; but in this case, those who simply dislike a ratty old building, I think, can be accused of lack of imagination. Remember what San Miguel looked like before it was carefully and correctly restored, then imagine what a restored Nusbaum Building would be.

The second main group seems to consist of a rather small number of merchants who fear that their businesses will suffer if the city does not provide parking "within half a block of the plaza" (that is their key phrase) and who want the people of Santa Fe thus to subsidize them. The subsidy is unwarranted. So are the fears.

I don't know why a sudden fear should overwhelm a group of people that customers will no longer be willing to walk a block or two to their stores. People always have done so, they do it now — why should they stop? In big cities they walk a lot farther.

If, say, I want a certain kind of jacket, I'll walk to Moore's; for another garment, to Goodman's, while the hardy souls who seek out all the bargains will walk many blocks to Levine's perennial sales.

Dendahl's has put the finger on an important formula. Make it attractive around your shop. Make it agreeable to come there. Then people will park by the federal building and come your way to enjoy a stroll. The critical word here is "enjoy." If merchants on and close to the plaza fear that it will lose its business, they should be thinking about making it a walkway and developing attractions such as open-air eating and refreshment facilities. Periodically our grocery stores put on free circuses to attract trade. Dealers in less perishable goods should consider more permanent attractions, at no cost to themselves.

We are warned, also, that if the Nusbaum Building goes

down,* we may lose the Prince buildings, which would be a catastrophe. We can require that new buildings comply with certain style requirements. Fine. But pull out all the really old ones, everything that really backs up the city's claim to age, authenticity, and a special culture, and pretty soon it will look like a mouthful of false teeth, with a single old molar, the Governors' Palace, in one corner. Nobody, but nobody, will cross the continent just to look at a well-constructed set of dentures.

* It did go down. A parking lot now graces the site.

Nine Cents and the Machine

W RITING PIECES critical of the Public Service Company is like shooting sitting ducks. Any public utility, I imagine, is bound to cause some annoyance and induce a sense of public futility; one that has become a captive of the IBM machines is an almost hopeless case. But today is hot and depressing again; after too many similar days, it is tempting to take the easy way out, and an item has been handed to me too good not to share.

One of the up and coming art galleries around here is 626 Canyon Road. The talented group of painters who set it up are trying to run it as a business proposition, and so far they have been doing a pretty nice business — with good reason, as anyone who inspects their wares will agree.

Within a few days after the 626 Gallery opened, it became official, received its baptism, one might say, in the form of one of those fast bills. The bill puzzled the treasurer. He made out the date all right, and what seemed to be the account number, but only after long consideration did he conclude that a single numeral, 9, floating around the southeast corner, was what the Gallery owed.

It was not 9., nor .90, nor .09; it was graced neither by $ nor by c. It was just 9. Nine what? Anyway, it was early in the month, the Gallery was just beginning to take in money, this sudden billing — against a $15 deposit — seemed obviously out of line. He put the bill aside.

With his well-known, new speed, Mr. Kilowatt sent a past due notice. It was stacked with the other, to wait the other bills that would be sent in according to usual business procedure, on the first of the month. The first was hardly past, the recent commissions from sales hardly deposited, when in rushed the third bill, the one that carries that rigmarole about how "we shall assume our services are no longer wanted" or however it goes, and the company will jolly well cut off your water and lights if you don't come across.

The treasurer took the three slips, unbent, unspindled, unwritten upon, to the Public Service Company office. He ascertained that the amount due was indeed nine cents, and he paid the same in cash. This payment exactly equalled the postage paid by the ever-eager, faster company. Who took care of the overhead, the wear and tear on the machines, or the cost of envelopes and other materials, we know not.

What we know is that down in Albuquerque are a lot of strangely deft, senseless machines, mechanically committing imbecilities upon a frustrated public. Machines can stamp numbers all over a piece of cardboard, and cut holes in it that will tell other machines how to commit further stupidities with it. Machines cannot think. They care nothing for public opinion, and no matter how deft and intricate they may be, they are incapable of simple common sense. Being enslaved to them is like being enslaved to an industrious monkey.

On the whole, we are not yet enslaved to our machines. The people have a fine careless humanity to them that insists upon behaving with reason, humor, good sense, and irregularity. If one of our utilities insists upon spending unnecessary sums of money on postage and this peculiarly unattractive form of stationery, most of the people will say "let it spend."

They will continue to pay their bills at the usual time, in

the usual way. There is, as a matter of fact, something pathetic in the picture of those machines, so ingeniously created by human brains, clattering away day after day, sending out unreasonable and senseless notices — PAST DUE — we shall assume — wasting the company's money. Be it $5 covered by a $10 deposit, or 9¢ covered by $15, or by $30, they will still follow up, still automatically call for postage, and then, when the payment is made, the payment from which the automatons have already stripped a percentage of the profit, the machines will clatter again, laboriously recording the fact, adding up totals, spouting yet other cards.

How much waste mechanical energy of this kind goes on in the United States, I wonder? How much invention, technical skill, and knowledge, is squandered on devices for doing the unnecessary? How many Americans think that merely because the machine has speed enough to perform useless functions, it is "progress" to cause those functions to be performed?

Man started making tools in order to make life easier. The function of the machine, an elaborate form of tool, is the same. But like the ancient pagans, we worship the gods we ourselves have made. The machines are brisk, marvelous to watch in action, and make an impressive clatter. Impressed, we admire them and let them run on, oblivious to the fact that all this noise and motion is only sound and fury, a form of raving, the mechanization of idiocy — unless we ourselves, the humans, the thinkers, dominate, guide, and control our machines.

Wearing Down the Gas Company

I HAVE HEARD A fascinating story of a lady here in Santa Fe who claims that it is largely because of her that the gas company took to envelopes. The story is too good not to share, so I recite it here as I heard it, for what it may be worth and for the delectation of all.

The lady in question, a strong-minded and attractive female, is in revolt against the principle of open-faced billing by anybody. As I understand it, she made inquiries at the post office, and found that, in fact, a statement of someone's indebtedness on a postcard, for others who happen to handle the mail to see, may be contrary to regulations.

She then thought up a fiendishly simple and simply fiendish device. If the utilities can bill by postcard, why cannot the customers pay in the same way? Under what obligation, if any, are the customers, to return that postcard at all? After all, she reasoned, if you show your account number on the check, the company in question can jolly well look your account up in the books and see if the payment is correct.

This called for more inquiry at the post office. Her new point was whether there was any rule, regulation, or law that says that a check is ineligible to be handled as a postcard. The authorities scratched around, read those fat books of fine print by which the postal system is governed, and did a bit of hemming and hawing. The idea, after all, was quite new.

The upshot of all their study was that, no, there was nothing that said that a check could not be a postcard, or a post-card a check. Of course, the sender would have to take a certain chance on the check's being torn in transit. As to that, if you mail the check in the same post office in which it is delivered, and above all where it goes into a box, the chances that it will get through in negotiable form are good.

So she wrote out her check, put her account number on the face of it, addressed the back to the gas company, stuck on a postage stamp, and mailed it.

It worked. As I heard the tale, she passed the word to a number of her friends, who gleefully joined in her operation. This, as one can plainly see, meant a novel and genuine harassment of the company. The checks would arrive with postmarks and such on their backs; they would, I am sure, often be somewhat crumpled, and in each case someone at the company's office would have to look up the account.

This procedure, she proudly claims, was what wore down the gas company. If correct, she has a right to be proud. Now, I am informed, she is starting work on our old friend Reddy Kilowatt of the faster bills.

Please note that I make no guarantee of this story. Nor do I recommend that my readers emulate the lady. I have not checked with the post office; I had meant to do that, but various circumstances have prevented me, and the story is past due to be told.

Anyhow, I don't really believe in cruelty to public utilities; I just like to see them suffer. This attitude is one of the cornerstones of American democracy. The telephone company now sends two bills, in an envelope, with a return envelope, and nowadays with a clearly intelligible listing of toll calls. It would be nice if the Public Service Company would join the parade.

Some Folklore and a Monument

From several sources I hear of a peculiar folklore of misinformation about the obelisk in the center of the plaza. It is important that the truth be made known, for, I hope, the fine drive that the Caballeros de Vargas are showing will lead to raising the funds necessary for erecting the De Vargas statue, and the nature of the central monument bears upon the difficult matter of the statue's location.

One false belief is that the monument landed in the plaza because it was unwanted and there was nowhere else to stick it. This is obviously absurd. The monument was authorized by the territorial legislature to celebrate the outcome of two serious wars, its cornerstone was laid in November, 1867, with great pomp and ceremony, and it was carefully placed in the most honorable spot in New Mexico, in the center of the capital's plaza, fronting what was then both the governor's mansion and the territorial capitol.

The other is that this monument celebrates Anglo-American achievements and has no meaning to Spanish-Americans. This belief is also entirely false; its currency shows that too many of our Spanish-Americans have forgotten a proud chapter in their own history.

The monument is dedicated on two sides to those who died in the Civil War fighting for the Union, on the third side to those who died fighting "savage Indians," meaning Navahos and Apaches.

Both wars were fought simultaneously. At the beginning of the Civil War, the bulk of regular army troops were withdrawn, to be replaced by volunteers. In short order New Mexico found itself in a pincers movement, with the Confederate forces striking from the southeast, the Navahos from the northwest, and the Mescaleros operating in between. Had the volunteer federal forces been recruited only from Anglos, there would hardly have been enough to make a company. The bulk of the forces were Spanish-American, not only the enlisted men but the officers, of whom the highest was Lt. Col. J. Francisco Chaves.

The Spanish people must have volunteered the more readily in that they were old enemies of the Navahos and Apaches, and that the Confederate troops who invaded New Mexico were from Texas. For whatever reason, volunteer they did, fought bravely against the "rebels," and provided the manpower that defeated them at Glorieta.

They went on, fighting equally bravely under Chaves, Kit Carson, and others, in the long and difficult campaigns that pacified both the Mescaleros and the powerful Navahos, against whom the efforts of regulars had been unavailing for years.

On February 6, 1864, *The New Mexican* reported, "We have often, and with much pleasure, received warm recommendations from officers of the regular army, in favor of the patience, good order, and discipline of volunteer (Spanish-American) soldiers. . . . Travel and campaigns seem natural to them. The soldiers of the first regiment are said to have improved since the first day they were mustered into service. They have recently done excellent service in the Navajos country. . . . These men deserve high credit and consideration. . . ."

Most of these men were born citizens of Mexico. In a time

of crisis they showed how completely they had adopted the United States. In the campaigns of 1862–1866 they established a glorious tradition which they have continued in full force in the Spanish-American War, when they poured into the Rough Riders, the two World Wars, and the Korean War.

This, then, is what that little monument stands for. It commemorates loyalty, courage, and victory, the first positive joint action of the English and Spanish peoples of New Mexico to serve their country, with the Spanish in the leading role, the beginning, to repeat, of a great tradition.

I can see why a Texan might not be fond of this monument. A Southerner or a Navaho might object to "rebel" and "savage" — expressions of the time, mementos of the honest feelings of that age. To the Spanish-Americans, it should be one of their most cherished monuments, for it is they, above all, whom it celebrates.

Newcomers might well be confused, but I am surprised that an old-timer such as Spud Johnson should think for a moment that the "savage Indians" referred to so sincerely on the north side of the monument meant the Pueblos. So far as I know, hostilities with the Pueblos ended not long after the bloody (not "bloodless" as so often advertised) reconquest of New Mexico by De Vargas. From then until the Navahos were broken and signed the Treaty of 1868, Santa Fe and all New Mexico, including the Pueblos, were relentlessly harried, threatened with extinction, many settlements and pueblos wiped out, by Navahos, Apaches, Kiowas, and Comanches.

Those were the "savage Indians." No one even faintly conversant with New Mexico history could doubt to whom the territorial legislature was referring, or forget that Pueblo Indians were among the "heroes" who fought against them and are commemorated on that slab.

Under the Madison Avenue influence, we are getting to

where we want even our history made bland, sweetened,
suited for consumption without any sensation whatsoever.
The plaza monument is something else again, an authentic
survival of frontier days, of the emotions of those times, of
their simplicity and even of their crudity.

You can, of course, prefer to raze the Sena and Prince Patios and the Governors' Palace, replacing them with smoothly
designed and packaged buildings such as surround most of
our central square. You can decide to bury all traces of what
Santa Fe once was and forget that New Mexico's history was
full of storms and violence. Personally, I prefer to keep a little of the real thing, to counterbalance the next ballet of
whiskers and poke bonnets when we confuse our anniversaries
with those of Square Corners, Ioway.

The monument refers to "savage Indians," it means exactly what it says, and furthermore, the term is accurate.
That the white men, in fighting them, were often equally savage is beside the point. I know of no recorded case of the
Comanches killing anyone with kindness.

The monument refers to "Rebels" in the same forthright
manner. To many Civil War veterans who looked upon the
monument with satisfaction, the word in their minds must
have been "Tejanos." The common people of New Mexico
were bitterly anti-Texan, hence devotedly pro-Union.

On the monument are several errors, one of which, the
misspelling of February, has attained national fame. On the
west side, someone got the date of the Battle of Peralta wrong,
or misspelled April, so that the name of the month was cut
out and recarved. On the north side, something went wrong
with Heroes, and it, too, had to be done over.

The carver was probably Spanish-American, working in a
language he did not speak. This was the frontier, and slabs of
marble were hard to come by. This was the frontier, and even

the Anglos, perhaps even Chief Justice Slough, who was so soon to be shot dead in the lobby of La Fonda, did not notice the misspelling of February.

Very shortly after the monument was dedicated, vandals stole the coins out of the cornerstone of the new Cathedral that Archbishop Lamy had just laid. This was the frontier.

The monument is authentic, it is unpretentious, it is a true record of an important passage in New Mexico history. It is altogether too easy to brush such simple things aside, brushing our predecessors aside along with them, in favor of a Madison Avenue version, chocolate-peppermint flavored for tourist consumption.

For heaven's sake, you who want to keep a little of the real Santa Fe, resist every move to remove those stones as you would resist having the bones of your ancestors ground into fertilizer for the capitol gardens.

The Season of Fiesta

THIS PIECE is being written in the calm before Zozobra, but it will appear in mid-Fiesta.* This is the season of the maximum influx of visitors to Santa Fe, and also the season when the inhabitants of the Ancient City and environs let down their hair and act completely natural (i.e. slightly loony), just like the City Council. For the benefit of those visitors who, on Sunday, may still be able to read fairly fine print, we shall explain a few things about Santa Fe and New Mexico that may have been puzzling them.

The name "Santa Fe" is pronounced "Santa Fay," and not "Santerfee." It is not correct to put an accent on the "e." It is a Spanish, not a French name.

Santa Fe is the capital of New Mexico, and New Mexico, many of our visitors will be disappointed to hear, is one of the fifty states of the Union. United States money is accepted here at face value — in fact, it is accepted avidly. You will not have to submit to a customs inspection or pay duty on the things you may buy here, unless possibly if you enter the Republic of Texas.

New Mexico is part of the United States, but it is not part of Texas. Texas is much longer and wider than New Mexico, but the latter state is a great deal thicker. Rhode Island is smaller, wetter, and has clams, while New Mexico is high and dry, and has tamales, hence the atomic bomb.

* Its annual date corresponds to Labor Day weekend.

Santa Fe is very old and hence the streets are very tired. It is an old Spanish custom to apologize to a street when you bump over a rut. That rut may well have been started by one of De Vargas' men trailing his pike as he walked along. Treat it with respect. If you don't, it will bust your springs for you.

The Spanish-speaking people of Santa Fe are not Mexicans. They differ from Mexicans physically, in manner of speech, and in customs. They have fought for the United States in every war since, and including, the Civil War.

The Indians you see peddling their wares are not subsidized by the Chamber of Commerce or Fred Harvey. They are independent entrepreneurs and exemplify the rugged individualism and personal enterprise so valued by all good Republicans.

The government of this city is strictly nonpartisan, a curious fact since all members of the City Council are staunch adherents of either the Republican or the Democratic party. Regardless of party affiliation, the majority party always defends the status quo and is particularly quick to fight off any attempt to meddle with the police force, while the minority party always battles vainly for a long list of reforms. This has been going on for 250 years, and is another old Spanish custom.

The state Republican party has a habit of nominating ex-mayors of Santa Fe for governor or lieutenant-governor, or both. This is because any man optimistic enough to accept the position of mayor of this madhouse will be game for almost anything. The Democrats then snow the candidate under, especially on the East Side. This is an old Texas custom.

The "Mexican" food that you may eat while you are here is not Mexican. It is local. Along the border, you find some similar dishes, but they are not identical. As you get well into Mexico the cuisine changes radically. A few dishes do remain pretty well constant; among these are chocolate and tamales, the consumption of which on festive occasions is an old Aztec custom. The Aztecs learned it from the Toltecs, the Toltecs learned it from the Mayas, and the Mayas learned it from the Old Santa Fe Association.

The first person to put a marshmallow in Mexican-style chocolate was Doña Encarnación Cantando y Bailando de Paniagua in 1884. She did it with the simple and reasonable intention of poisoning a deputy sheriff, instead of which she nourished and delighted him (thus achieving much the same ultimate end) and established a new Spanish custom.

All visitors are very welcome to Fiesta. We hope they will enjoy themselves as much as we enjoy watching their picturesque costumes and their interesting customs. The idea is for everyone to have a good time and feel at home. This is also an old Spanish custom.

Beginning in June, a pleasant form of madness begins seeping through Santa Fe, growing ever more apparent as we move through the summer towards the ultimate, uninhibited outbreak of Las Fiestas. It is correlated with the constantly increasing flood of visitors, which may not quite engulf us all, but leaves few unspattered.

Writers and artists, at least, as I can testify, find it almost a law of nature that as soon as they become really immersed in a piece of work, there will arrive at their door an Egyptian architect with State Department credentials, a French priest of literary inclinations, an administrator from the Belgian Congo, or a Siamese sociologist, bearing letters of introduction. These visitors almost always prove too interesting to be brushed off lightly, and another day goes down the drain.

The visitors themselves seem to be progressively more daffy as Fiesta time approaches. They are somewhat more possessed by the mood of Santa Fe. The rate of social life steps

up; there is always something going on. In this period almost
anything can happen, and usually does.

The other day I was driving along the Old Pecos Road
(which, please note, is not the present road to Lamy). Where
the road dips to cross the Arroyo Chamiso, I saw a car, off
the roadbed in the sand. It was a sedate-looking, four-door
sedan. Standing near the back of it, then, I descried three
nuns, who appeared to be digging.

Believing that the devoted ladies were in trouble, I slowed
down. Then I saw that all three of them were wielding long-
handled shovels, and all three were wearing blue and white
checked aprons over their dark habits. They were patiently
shoveling up sand and pouring it into the back of the car.
That, I thought, is Santa Fe, and I went on by, leaving them
to their occupation.

Now the weather-beaten men come down from Chimayo
and Trampas to sell cucumbers and chile verde. The feeling
of the end of summer is in the air, and children, smelling
school beyond the horizon, become subject to new urgencies.
The number of Indians under the portal of the Palace of the
Governors increases, and more of them are wearing their Indian suits. The hotels fill up, and the costumes of the visitors
become ever more curious.

You would not, in this season, be surprised to encounter a
laughing horse or a talking dog. It is obvious that something
is going to pop, and so it is fitting that at the end of summer,
and not at any other time, comes the outburst of Fiesta.

Its rites are many and curious, beginning with the unique
and wonderful creation of Zozobra.* (I suppose you can refer
to a destruction also as a creation.) There is the solemnity of
the candlelight procession. There are the peaceful charm and

* A towering monster, a type of Old Man Gloom, whose burning inaugu-
rates Fiesta.

real beauty of the Indian dances in the patio of the Governors' Palace, one of the most rewarding and certainly most authentic events of Fiesta.

In La Fonda many visitors and a sprinkling of local residents submit themselves to a curious form of self-immolation which derives, I believe, from the Sun Dance of the Plains Indians. They pack themselves into a semidarkened room, the air of which is swiftly exhausted, and there endure the most intense pangs of thirst. The Plains Indians, while enduring their thirst, used to add to their sacrifice by various forms of self-torture. The present celebrants, being more advanced, have invented a more refined form of torment. At very long intervals a harried ministrant hands one or another a beverage. It is just enough to maintain the urgent need for more, while the sight of its consumption agonizes the surrounding celebrants.

Today, Sunday, as happens every year, a number of visitors are discovering to their horror that no liquor can be had. This is the day when the proprietor of a bottle enjoys — or desperately wards off — a sudden popularity. Tomorrow Fiesta will wind up, leaving everyone a trifle haggard. The slow motion always characteristic of Santa Fe will return, but for a day or so it will be more pronounced. The silly season will taper away, the smell of piñon smoke will fill the streets again, there will be frost at night, there will be a new excuse for getting mad at the City Council. Santa Fe will return as near as it ever gets to sanity, and stay so — until the next time.

My aged friend the Horned Husband Kachina Chief from Awatovi turned up Friday morning, riding a burro and driving another, to attend Fiesta. Right after him his great-nephew arrived in a fan-tailed Chevy, and as the young man (he's not a day over fifty) speaks some English, communication between us was greatly facilitated. The Chief's remarks, as I record them here, are in his nephew's words.

"We come take in Fiestas," he told me. "Not seen Fiestas in many years."

"Welcome," I said. "I hope you have a lot of fun."

The nephew offered me a cigaret-sized cheroot. I refused with a shudder. The Chief held forth a small bag of tobacco they smoke in the kivas. I refused with two shudders.

"Plenty fun," the Chief said. "Too bad my great-nephew's littlest boy not here. He very smart, use camera. Take pictures of these picturesque white people. Why you all time change you native costume? You shamed or you can't make up your mind? One time, women all long skirt, no see leg, no see nothing but face and hair piled up on top. Next time, short, short skirt, little hair. Now, men and women in short pants, only way you tell women from men is, men wear stockings. Why you people never settle down?"

This was a question I preferred not to try to answer. Fortunately, the Chief became preoccupied with unpacking his burro. He is not the only friend I have who asks questions, not to get an answer, but as a way of making a remark.

"Inyan goods," he said, pointing to the materials he had placed on the ground.

"Some from Woolworth's," I commented. "Is that a new tribe?"

"Five-and-dime and Inyans natural cousins," he said. "These here, dozen my nephews and two grandsons make 'em. Buy one at five-and-dime, then copy 'em." The great-nephew interpolated on his own. "We so good now, we make machine-made goods by hand."

"They won't let you sell that stuff at the Indian market."

"All right; we paddle it. Over here —" he opened a bundle full of really fine Indian stuff, "make Inyan Arts Fund happy."

The Chief bummed a cheroot off his nephew. "Save my tobacco to smoke in Fiesta kiva," he explained.

"Fiesta kiva?"

"Yes. In La Fonda. Lots people come Santa Fe, go in retreat La Fonda today, not come out till Tuesday. Only some get swep' out. I sit in there, make cloud medicine with pipe, then come out, watch Inyans dance in Governors' Palace. Like that change around. Very nice?"

"Aren't you getting into the parade?" I asked. "You've got a nice outfit."

The Chief was silent. The great-nephew said in a low voice, "His feet hurt."

The old man spoke in an indignant tone.

"He say, this white people show. Anglo people, Spanish people, more fun he sit and watch. Plenty time at home he amuse white people; he come here for them amuse him, make him laugh."

That made sense. I nodded.

"Time now to go plaza, eat samwich with hamburger, green chili, tomato, onion. Fill up on vitamin. Three good chili samwiches give you vitamin for all winter. Then go see Zozobra burn. See you later."

The last glimpse of the old Chief I had was Saturday afternoon at the Indian dances. He had been making cloud medicine like mad in the Fiesta kiva, and the fresh air, the cool grass, the familiar rhythm of the dances had overcome him. He was fast asleep on a valuable Navaho blanket, in one hand an unfinished green chili hamburger, in the other an elegant copy of a mass-produced totem pole that he had purchased from a visiting Eskimo.

II

Writing
the Language

The Man with
the Calabash Pipe: V

A CHILL, puffy west wind was blowing out of a purple-brown
and mustard yellow cloud bank that hid the Jemez Mountains and much of the western sky. It felt like snow coming.
I found the Man with the Calabash Pipe in his armchair,
close up against the fire in his book-walled study. A likeable
mouse, he explained, lived under his heater, and he was reluctant to turn it on.

He had laid his pipe aside to scan the evening paper. (He
had experimented once, for nearly a year, with homeopathy,
and ever since, out of sentiment, subscribed to *The Abiquiu
Times*.) He waved me to a seat, then picked up his pipe and
filled it slowly. His expression was sad.

He then tore a wide strip out of the middle of the front page
of his paper, rolled it into a spill, and used it to light his pipe.

"I should think you'd finish reading before you started to
burn it up," I said.

"I have," he answered sadly, "scanned the headlines, as
the phrase goes. It is a dubious habit, but hard to break once
formed. At times it leads to a nausea that prevents further
perusal."

"As for instance?"

"As for instance," he gestured with the stem of his pipe towards the smouldering remains of the spill, "I have just cre-
mated a headline that read, 'Solons Mull Brit-Russ Pact.'" He
shuddered. After a good long drag at his pipe, he regained

strength. "Repulsive and meaningless though such a headline is, I made myself read far enough to find out what the
news actually was — if you can call it news. A couple of
minor congressmen want to know more about a possible
British-Soviet trade agreement. Which, interpreted, meaneth,
a couple of minor congressmen were hard up for newspaper
mention, and have now achieved it."

He puffed his pipe back to life. "Headline-writing has become a thing done for its own sake, and no longer for the benefit of the reader. The craft of it is to pack the appearance of
a lot of meaning into a very few, large letters. I am speaking,
not of the principal headlines, the purpose of which is to sell
the paper and call your attention to the big news of the hour,
but of the minor ones. Very few letters are allowed. The result is frightful, unintelligible, often misleading."

He cleared his throat, "Solon was the great law-giver of ancient Greece — as I suppose you know." He glanced at me
suspiciously. "To call a man 'a solon' used to mean that he,
too, was the author of wise, important laws. Because of headlines, the word now means anyone connected with any legislature."

He made another spill and relit his pipe. "Let's just forget
about 'pact.' It is a synonym for neither treaty nor agreement,
a good word that now one avoids using. 'Mull,' of course, expresses a slow, dull way of thinking, possibly even muddled,
undoubtedly appropriate in this case, but not what the writer
intended."

"Isn't it possible," I put in, "that the boys are indulging
in a little sarcasm whenever they use that word?"

"Possible, but unlikely." He did not like having his flow
of speech interrupted; now he got up steam again. "The word
'Russ' for Russian had some currency between the time of
King Henry VIII and the middle of the eighteenth century.

In reviving it, the headline writers have at least stayed within the limits of the English language, and on the whole are even using the word in its actual meaning — a rarity. Whoever, thereafter, coined 'Brit' as a sort of companion was guilty of pure mayhem. That word never existed, even in slang, like 'Jap.' No doubt in due course we shall get 'Its' for Italians, 'Ams' for Americans — as though we were a religious movement, not a nation — and 'Germs' for Germans."

He leaned forward and shook his pipe at me. "No doubt," he said in tones of horror, "some ill-inspired headline writer will start referring to 'Solons' as 'Sols.'"

Moodily, he fell to tearing the whole paper into strips and rolling them into spills. In the quiet, I could hear his likeable mouse chewing softly on a leather-bound edition of *Religio Medici*.

Criticism and
the Experience of Writing

A CURIOUS, small controversy on the subject of artists and criticism has been going on in the columns of this paper. If I read them aright, one correspondent avers that there should be no criticism, since the actual value of a work of art can be determined only down the ages, and that all that a critic — or art commentator — should do is encourage all who struggle, while another claims that there is no room for question about our living greats; there they are and already destined for the ages.

Both points of view strike this writer as in error. We commonly speak of "artists and writers," but writing is generally acknowledged as an art, and a thoughtful writer is as conscious as any artist is — or, rather, ought to be — of the labile nature of the attribution of greatness. I say "attribution," because what determines greatness, other than in the minds of the self-satisfied, is the opinion of a work held by an informed public.

Blake was little honored in his time; today he has become one of the great poets. Early nineteenth century poets and critics accepted Leigh Hunt as the best of all; today he is forgotten. Melville and Walt Whitman have steadily grown with the generations, but *Hiawatha* has become a joke, and who today reads William Dean Howells?

Looking back over the long course of the art of writing, we do see a few who seem to have been great in their time and ever since. Shakespeare wrote smash hits which continued to be read and played — but for two centuries after his death it was the common practice to rewrite him drastically to make him less crude.

Horace, on finishing his third book of poems, wrote, "I have raised up a monument more lasting than bronze," and so long as any knowledge of Latin continues it looks as if he will prove correct. I wonder, however, whether the next generation after his did not consider him rather quaint and old-fashioned.

So we have no way of knowing which, if any, of our recent greats will stand up under the test of time, be it Picasso or Tennessee Williams, Epstein or Hemingway. We know that we esteem them great, and with that we — and they — must be content.

In writing thus, I do not intend to offer any aid or comfort whatsoever to those who condemn current criticism just because today's critic can no more see into the next century than today's artist or today's buyer. To argue that there should be no criticism, only encouragement, is to ask for an acquiescent silence that would be deadly.

The errors of critics confronting new art, new writing, are historic. Even these errors created stimulating controversy. To be a good artist in any field, one must have character, the character to withstand poverty and discouragement, to resist hostile criticism and fight back at it, not by screaming shrilly, but by doing one's work so well that in time it will prove its own case, and, the most difficult of all, to take to heart and profit by unfavorable criticisms when these are soundly made.

Modern creative artists are often spoiled. They write, and are published, without competence in their native language; they paint, and are exhibited, without any rigors of training. This is not universal, but too common. Their education has probably contained a large element of "life adjustment" courses and they have been graded noncompetitively. There will always be some who can't stand criticism, but among those for whom the road to public appearance has been made so easy, the proportion is bound to be extra high.

I once read a ghastly story about a world in which sickness and old age had been abolished; people simple dropped dead when their appointed time came, no one knew when it would be, no one knew why, everyone lived in fear. An artist's world without critics would be somewhat similar. No art columns, no book reviews, no expressions of opinion. Your work is hung, placed on a pedestal, or published and there are no purchasers, and no one will tell you anything except "keep trying." There's a nightmare for you!

It is well known that writers are poor judges of their own work. Some years ago a number of big names were asked to select from their own stories the one they thought best, the selection then being published as an anthology. Critical opinion was about unamimous that they chose poorly. Inability to judge one's own work is doubled when the work is new. A sufficient lapse of time can separate the writer from his product, as it were, and enable him to judge it without paternal (or is it maternal?) bias.

This comes home to me at this moment, because I have been spending a number of days overhauling boxes of manuscripts and printed sheets torn from magazines, to see what was worth keeping. It has been rather a depressing experience.

I had a feeling that in the course of recent years I had turned out a lot of good work. I remembered the sense of satisfaction I had with one finished job after another, the renewed satisfaction when, later, I reread them in the formality and majesty of print. No question, print does things for a story. Once I had read the things in print, I filed them away, and never looked at them again until now, so nothing had occurred to overcome that first flush of satisfaction. Reread after five, ten, or more years, they certainly look different.

A professional story-writer usually makes it his rule to write every story that occurs to him unless he sees that it is definitely no good. He writes it as well as he knows how, even though he knows it to be "slight," or "unimportant," or "merely popular." Many a mediocre idea can be turned into a source of pleasure by good writing.

The result is that he has put a lot of effort and feeling into the product. He is not going to like the idea of throwing it away. He has developed a prejudice in favor of it. Also, he is in business. His art, his delight, is writing; his business is selling. So he sends the thing out and hopes for luck.

Five years later, the various, rather complex efforts and emotions involved in the act of writing far in the past, he picks up the story cold. The creative love for it has faded. Then comes the unpleasant realization that this really was a poor job.

Then there are the stories that never did get published. Some of them were written out of pure love. He felt that they were really nifty. Publication has never rung the curtain down on them and some of his original, defiant feeling that this one and this one were really fine and that editors are a dumb lot remains.

I have one piece that has been rejected by everything from *The Saturday Evening Post* to the *New Mexico Quarterly*. Common sense tells me that the unanimous opinion of so many and so different editors can't be wrong. The story must be a turkey. The other day I reread it three different times. I still love it. Why? What's the matter with whom? Is this an example of a writer talking to himself, saying something that has adequate meaning to himself only? I don't know. It's a

queer business all around. The things you feel surest of at the
time of writing proceed to lay eggs, the off piece that you
doubted is the one that gets across, and what will look well
after five years is unpredictable.

The moment of sending off a book is a strange one. I don't
know too much about how other writers feel, but it's my impression that most of them feel an emptiness at that point.

Writing a book takes nearly a year. If you are lucky, during
that period you do virtually no other work; you just live in
the book. More likely, you break off the big job from time to
time to write a story, or an article that's been ordered, or to attend to any one of the many other forms of work that are a
writer's bread and butter. Even so, you carry the thought of
the book with you, and keep returning to it. It is more than
an occupation; it is a special sort of life.

It has a two-fold hold on the writer. Fiction, narrative non-
fiction, history, biography, all have characters, plot, beginning,
ending, and a climax of some sort. They have a background
or setting. There is the development not only of the principal
characters but of the minor ones, who usually are, or should
be, far more completely worked out in the writer's mind than
appears in the finished book. Not a few writers take the time
to write brief, biographical outlines of almost all their characters, so as to give them depth.

So here is a whole imaginary world. It may be a familiar
world, derived from observed, present reality and close to it,
but it is broken off from the real world. Inside this, the writer
must move, observe, respond. He does not arbitrarily control
it, although it is his creation. If his imagining has been
sound, if his characters are "real," his situations credible, in
short order a definite logic, a necessary sequence of causes and
effects, of inevitable reactions of certain characters to situations, takes control. What then goes on is fascinating and
sometimes surprising.

In addition to this imaginary world, this second, inner life, the writer is busy with his art, like any other artist. There is nothing imaginary about the technical problems that arise and must be successfully solved or about the need for constant self-criticism and tough appraisal of what he has just done. For a man who loves his work, this aspect of it is as enthralling as the imaginary side.

He makes a first draft, relaxes, lets it cool off, then he revises. In the revision he returns to both absorptions, with a greater emphasis on the technical side, and he stays with it again when he retypes, or puts the thing in final shape for a typist, and then gives it final reading.

Now he must wrap it up and ship it. Of course, if you asked him, he'd say that his principal reason for writing it was to get it published; yet it's almost painful to let it go. Then it will be read by an editor whom he probably knows slightly, various subeditors whom he does not know at all, and discussed at sales conferences by men whose eyes are strictly on business. As a usual thing he already has his contract and knows that the book will be printed; what he cannot know is what decision those unknown people have arrived at, that this book is a seller and should be pushed, or that it's not hot, and there's no use spending any more money on it than is absolutely necessary. His work of art, as James Stephens wrote, must go down into the market place and be judged by the gombeen men.

He sends it off, and then there is nothing more he can do about it except make some minor revisions when he gets the galley proofs. He'd better keep the revisions on the minor side, too, as virtually all contracts provide that if author's revisions exceed a certain cost, they will be charged to the author — and few authors can afford to support the members of the typographers' union.

It's a funny feeling, wrapping up and shipping the brain

child. The feeling existed long before the days of printing; it inspired Horace to end his first book with that ode to the book itself, which most of us are unable to do. There it goes. There will be the galleys eventually, then the long waiting, the reviews (you hope), the report of advance sales, and finally, in somewhat less than two years, the report of the first six months' sales. Not until then will you know whether you have rung the bell or just plain missed.

Most people, I believe, think of writing as a noisy craft, not that it literally makes noises — the average writer, indeed, insists furiously on silence all about him when at work. The common use of typewriters has raised the occupation a decibel or two, and there is always the possibility of a hearty curse when a sentence goes totally wrong; but by and large writing is not an occupation that annoys the neighbors, like riveting, playing the trombone, or staging cat fights.

It seems noisy in that the writer is continually putting out words to be laid before the public gaze. Much of the time, these words deal with anything but the writer himself, it is true in only a remote sense that "most writing is autobiographical," and despite the transient phenomena of the beat generation, very little writing worth reading is "self-expression." To himself, a writer does not seem noisy. Much of the time he feels as if he operated in a soundless vacuum.

Your best products may be exposed to the public, and elicit nothing but a resounding silence. Occasionally someone will speak to you about something you've had in a magazine or other periodical, but even this happens seldom enough so that it's positively a pleasure to be attacked. At least that proves that you've been read and taken seriously.

When you have produced a book there is usually a brief period of fuss. The advance copies arrive, the actual, physical books with your name on them, and I must admit that after all these years I still get a poke out of that. When I received my first copy of my first book, the solid fact of it, the unbelievable yet undeniable reality, had me walking on air all the rest of that day.

Then the book is out. You may sneak past booksellers' windows to see what sort of break they are giving you. Your idea of proper treatment is to have all windows filled with nothing but copies of your opus, accompanied, perhaps, by enlargements of a few critical raves, so you are disappointed, but not surprised. There are reviews. (If there are no reviews, I imagine you cut your throat.) The bad reviews are written by stupid asses, the good ones by perceptive, sensitive critics. Surprising how few good critics there are in the world.

There may be an autographing party, which will be attended by your most loyal friends plus three voluntary customers. Then silence closes over again, the fun is done, and you sweat out the royalty statement. You may have a reason to know that this or that book still sells, but you don't see it happen. Unlike a painter, you cannot walk into a museum and see your work hanging on the wall, or admire it from time to time when you enter someone's house. Most writers do snoop bookshelves when they go visiting, but they do it surreptitiously, and often in vain.

Every so often something happens that makes you feel as if your voice did, as a matter of fact, occasionally reach wide. Within the last week or so, for instance, a man I never heard of before wrote to me from Honduras about an article I'd written, and on the heels of that, an acquaintance in the East forwarded me a letter from an Italian lady who wrote enthusiastically about a book of mine she had read in the U. S. Information Library.

For a moment this kind of thing makes you feel that writing is what you thought it was when you were young, what

Horace and others such said it was. The sense of glamour returns. You feel that when you smite your lyre it will sound in far places, and you remember that reading, also, is a silent occupation. Writing is bread and butter in return for doing what one loves; little things like this are the lagniappe, the pâté de foie gras on top, and the taste is very good when it comes.

The Man with
the Calabash Pipe: VI

IN THE LATTER part of an afternoon, one is likely to find the Man with the Calabash Pipe as close to supine as it is possible to get in an armchair, eyes closed, meditating upon whatever he has been reading in the book that rests on his knees. On my last visit, however, I found him wandering about his room, his pipe unlit in his hand, no book on the table by his chair.

He gestured towards a chair, then pushed the humidor of the dreadful shag he chooses to smoke slightly towards me by way of invitation. I took out my own pouch, whereupon he gave his first sign of normality when he accepted a fill from it. He thanked me in a distracted manner and sank uneasily into his chair.

He stared into the bowl of his pipe, match in hand, and murmured, "Neither a lender nor a borrower be, because this too, too solid flesh may melt, And smoke gets in your eyes . . ."

Uneasily I said, "Have you a fever?"

"No, it's just a bad seizure of turning lines."

I did a double take internally, then remembered that in his youth he had spent some time in the theatre and had been, I believe, quite a success in the role of one of Laocoön's sons in the living statues. The phrase "turning lines" was a reminiscence of that period.

The match he pensively held in his right hand was about to burn his fingers — he was that distrait — so I leaned forward, blew it out, and offered him another. He lit up.

"I went to an appointment the other day, arriving on the dot, but my friend was not ready for me, and came out saying that punctuality was the thief of time. Before I knew what I was doing I told him that procrastination was the vice of princes. Then I passed a small boy on Acequia Madre, one of those dreadful, healthy, monkey-faced little creatures that you find barefoot on the covers of *The Saturday Evening Post*. They should go barefoot, and have their feet filled with tacks."

He leaned back in his chair and blew out smoke. "He was singing part of a song out of my youth, but the way he sang it, it ran, 'I've a ringworm round my shoulder . . .'" He shuddered.

"Furthermore," he said, "the other day I was in the company of some hip cats."

"Hep Cats," I said.

He waved his pipe at me. "No matter. Their language is infinitely corrupting. Do you know a sentimental ballad called 'Barbara Allan'?"

"Yes."

"Listen to this." He threw his head back, and, to my surprise — I had never heard him sing before — sang in an excellent baritone:

> "Oh father, father, dig my grave,
>   (Dig that crazy grave!)
> Oh dig it deep and narrow,
>   (Yeah man, it's square)
> Sweet William died for me today,
>   (He's cool, man, cool)
> I'll die for him tomorrow.
>   (Dig that crazy grave!)"

He relit his pipe. "I feel as if my reason were being unseated."

I said, "I don't blame you."

"The thing is a contagion," he said. "It extends to everything. Your wife was reading 'The Night before Christmas' to your child the other evening when I was there. All right, try this, in the light of the recent news:

"Now Dasher! Now Dancer! Now Jenner and Dirksen! On Comet! On Knowland! McCarthy and Nixon!"

He glared at me.

"To the top of the House —

"Of course it should be, to the top of the Senate, but it won't scan —

"So fade away, fade away, fade away, all! A happy Christmas wish, but imagine the screams of the children if Joe McCarthy turned up as Santa Claus."

I murmured, "A little phenobarbital —"

"I don't blame you. Those words have been running in my head, and I'd hate to have that kind of thing continue as the season of carols comes in."

Uneasily, I rose to go. He smiled at me wryly, and blew a great puff of smoke. "It's all right, really," he said. "I tell myself that on Christmas Day itself, it's not the gifts, it's the spirits that count."

On my way out, I closed the door sharply.

Hearing from the Public

NOTE: Any resemblance between the following letter and letters actually received by this writer is strictly intentional and malicious.

DEAR MR. LA FORGE:
I am a junior at Dumpleville High School. Our English teacher has told us to write a thesis about a well-known American writer, and I have chosen you. I went into the Public Library and looked at the names on the books on the shelves, and when I came to your books I remembered a cute story of yours that I read in *The Farm Wives' Home Companion* when I was in the dentist's office waiting to have my braces tightened and so I chose you.

Will you please send me a complete list of your writings, and also write me a biography of yourself. Please tell me why you started to write and how you like your career, also summarize your novels in your own words, and explain what message you were trying to convey in each of them. These last two questions are specially important as they are what our English teacher wants us to include in our themes.

Please also write some human facts about yourself, such as the most exciting incident of your life, your favorite flower, food, and drink, your hobby, and also send me an autograph

photo of yourself. I have a lot of pictures of people on televi-
sion, and I would like to put yours on the wall, too.

Yours sincerely,
AMELIA GLUTINUS

DEAR MISS GLUTINUS:
Thank you for your undated letter. I am flattered to know
that you have chosen to write your thesis about me, and I
hope it does not make your braces hurt. I wish you the best of
luck in your endeavor, and I am sorry that I cannot give you
the help you want.

I cannot do this in the first place because, if I did, your
English teacher might have me up for cheating. She wants
you to write a thesis, and although I can probably write a
better one on my favorite subject than you can, I don't think
she would like it. Then, I write for my living. What I write
I sell, or anyway try to sell. That is how that lousy story
about the noble girl with a heart of gold under her broken
nose finally landed in *The Farm Wives' Home Companion*.

That feeble publication pays only 200 bucks a story, and if
that one hadn't been a thorough turkey it never would have
landed there. I am sorry that you have to go to a dentist
who doesn't take anything better. You'd better have the vet
check your braces.

Now, I can write you an article on myself, and would gladly
do it, for the same price that was paid me by that magazine;
i.e. $200 prepaid. Or, if you can send me a certificate that
your local market has given you, free, a thick T-bone steak, a
pound of fresh mushrooms, a box of assorted chocolates, and
some aspirin tablets to give you strength for your scholarly
labors, and another from your stationer that he is providing
your pens, pencils, ink, paper, and erasers also for free, I'll see
if I can talk my agent into giving you a discount of 10 per cent.

You will be surprised to know it, but if you should make yourself read one of my books, you would find it written in pretty clear English, and you might be able to summarize it for yourself, and also you might find out what message, if any, I was trying to convey.

My favorite flower is the skunk cabbage, a nutritious and odoriferous plant which grows lavishly in my native Rhode Island. Another delightful bit of flora is the poison ivy, of which I should be happy to have my sister send you a bouquet. I cannot remember the most exciting incident of my life, as I was asleep when it happened. My hobby is sleeping. My favorite food is gin and bitters with a dash of tabasco and a float of lighted kerosene on top — you should try it over a banana split. It would do wonders for you. I have no favorite drink since, on account of my diet as described above, I have found drinking unnecessary.

I regret that I cannot send you a photograph of myself, because my wife tore up all we had in the house after the dog bit one and went into convulsions.

Hoping that this letter will assist you in your studies, and congratulating you on your selection, I remain,

Yours very sincerely
(and I mean sincerely)
WITCH DOCTOR LA FARGE

Miss Maebella Warple
24386 Manitou Vista Boulevard
Los Angeles 101, California

DEAR MISS WARPLE:
Thank you for your undated letter and kindly expressions about my novel *Laughing Boy*. It is particularly gratifying to know that you are now seriously considering spending 25¢ to

buy a soft-cover copy all your own. There is no surer proof of appreciation than the willingness to invest money in the article, and, as Somerset Maugham often says, we authors work at the command of royalties.

I am somewhat at a loss to know how to answer your question, "When are you going to give us another book?" In fact, I have been at a loss to know how to answer that one for some twenty years. It seems to be common knowledge that writers, like artists, do not work. Nonetheless, ethereal though we are, we have to eat — an item of information that may surprise you. As for our wives and children, their appetites are bottomless. On the other hand, they will not wear clothing that has become bottomless.

I do know a poet whose wife often goes barefoot, but then, poets are odd people and may be expected to have individualistic wives. In prose writers' families, the demand for raiment and shoes is incessant.

Under these circumstances, perhaps you can see that it would be difficult for even the most ethereal of us to live on the income derived from the occasional sale of the two-bit edition of an old book, which pays the author one cent per copy. After this explanation you may understand why in the course of the dreamy years since my first novel was published, I have written sixteen other books. I enclose herewith a list, with prices, and the addresses of several bookstores in your neighborhood, for your convenience.

You mention your desire to do a documentary film on the modern American Indians that will be different from the usual Hollywood product, that will tell their true story and will make the American public aware of the beauty of Indian life and the riches of Indian culture. I do wish you luck. It is my impression that 50 per cent of the adult population of the United States entertains the same idea. If all of those who are thinking of making such a film will pay to see the one that is finally made, the producer might break even.

I must warn you that, even though you explain your high purposes fully to whatever tribe you finally decide to film, the chances are that the people who act in your picture will want to be paid for so doing, and I fear that the full, correct performance of a major ceremony such as you hope for would be quite expensive. I doubt that, with an amateur cameraman and using 16 mm. film, you could make a profit. Indians, I fear, are almost as commercial as are writers.

Your suggestions for my participation are flattering. As I get it, you want me to decide on what reservation to do the shooting, rough out a story, find Indians to enact the main characters, spend several days with you filling you in on the facts of Indian life (since you have never had any direct contact with Indians), and accompany you to the reservation and advise you during the actual filming. You also hope I will supply dialog, as you say you have never been good at that.

Desiring to cooperate with you, I also attach hereto the name and address of my West Coast agent, who handles all cinema matters. You will find her experienced, clear-minded. She has an antipathy to any negotiation involving less than $5,000, which simplifies matters greatly.

All in all, if I am to have the pleasure of working with you, I think you had better raise some capital. You know, now that I think of it, I fear that authors are just as commercial as Indians.

Yours sincerely,
OLIVER LA FARGE

A Ban on *Laughing Boy*

I T WAS CURIOUS to learn, some days ago, that the first novel
I ever wrote had been removed from the libraries of the
public schools in Amarillo, Texas, on the grounds of obscenity. About a year ago I heard, through the protest of an irate
Southern lady who was quite unknown to me, that the same
book had been banned by a county school board in Georgia.
In that case, I gathered, the fundamental objection was to
my writing about a dark race — American Indians — as though
its members were as good as white men or sometimes better,
so the news merely amused me and saddened me somewhat
for what it showed about one bit of America.

Ever since I was young, I have wondered what it would
feel like to have someone rule that one's book was obscene.
Boston used to be the great city for it, and when I was beginning to write it was a cynical but practical observation that
getting the censors there to declare one's work immoral was an
excellent way to boost sales.

It seemed to me, and still does, that this is not the way I
would like to promote the sale of anything I had done. It certainly never occurred to me that it could happen to me. When
I thought about censorship, I thought about it as affecting me
only to the extent that it might prevent me from seeing or
reading works of art that I might think worthwhile.

Thus, I was shocked and annoyed to learn that there were
objections by local church authorities to the public showing

here of a film called *Never on Sunday*. This film had consistently high praise from all reviewers, had been much honored, is undoubtedly one of the few really good pictures made in the last year or so.

The heroine of *Never on Sunday*, like the heroine of my first novel, is not all she should be. My heroine's sins had a reason in the structure of the book, and it never crossed my mind that I could make my story juicy or sexy or more popular by exploiting them. I simply wanted a woman with a certain background, which would lead her into a certain error in her marriage.

The book came out in 1929 and was immediately followed by the stock market crash of that year. I do not believe that anyone has suggested that there was a connection between the two events. The book had a wide success, was published in foreign countries, and was made into a very poor movie. By the time it had been out ten years, I discovered that it was being used or recommended in college and high school English courses.

When I went to lecture or to do a spell of teaching at some college, it was a common experience to have students bring me copies of the paper-back edition to autograph. Some even had splurged and bought the hard cover version. All this has been most gratifying. The book has been in print now for more than thirty years. It has become old-fashioned and a bit dated, yet it still sells, and people much younger than I still tell me of their pleasure in it.

Naturally, the last thing I would expect, after all these years, was that a school board would find this novel obscene. And now it has happened. Now I know how it feels, insignificant though being banned in the schools of Amarillo (pop. 51,686) may be.

My first reaction was that some people on that school board

must have remarkably dirty minds. I still think that. Yet there is something else. I wrote that book with love, think of it with affection and pride, remembering an unworldly young man from whom I am descended and his quite pure pursuit of artistic beauty.

Now that work, that product of mine, in a real sense my unexpectedly successful child, has been smirched. It is a false smirching. It has no real meaning. Still, it has caused me a disagreeable sensation. I feel as if some nasty person had come up to me and drawn a slimy, unwashed finger across my hand. It is his dirt, not mine, but I would sooner not have been touched.

"Regional Writing"—Is What?

I HAVE BEEN ASKED to give a discourse on regional writing at the writers' conference at the University of Utah. In honesty I had to warn the authorities that, if my understanding of what "regional writing" means is correct, I'd have to talk against it. They said that that was all right.

But do I understand the meaning of the term? What is regional writing? A great many people speak favorably of it. Before trying to reach a firm opinion about it, we need to understand what it is.

We frequently hear it said that Faulkner, the Nobel prize winner, is our greatest regional writer. To me, if that term can be applied to Faulkner, then its scope is so broad as to be meaningless; virtually every book — or at least every novel — is then "regional."

We do not buy, or avoid, Faulkner's books because they are almost entirely laid in present-day Mississippi. We are not moved by interest in, or aversion to, the atmosphere and problems of the Deep South, although in reading his work we pick up a certain amount of knowledge of those things. His writing — not his potboilers, but the writing which has made his name — attracts or repels people for universal reasons. His technique, his use of stream of consciousness and internal monologue, his portmanteau words, his involuted sentences, substantially govern our judgments. More deeply, we find true or false, fascinating or unpleasant, his exposition of the inner well-springs of his characters, not as analyses of Mississippians, white or Negro, but as analyses of people.

Every story must in some way be placed in a locale and time. The pressures brought to bear upon the characters, their own mores, prejudices, and habits will be those of that placement; but our interest in them, our acceptance of their author as a true artist, will depend upon our acceptance of the characters, their emotions, their actions, as intelligible representations of mankind governed, in the end, by universal drives and inhibitions.

If the mere fact of choosing a single locale makes a book regional, which would seem to be what the inclusion of Faulkner among regional writers would indicate, then Dickens, Thackeray, Tolstoy even in *War and Peace*, are regional. Dickens, especially, concentrated heavily upon London as it was in his day. Does mere concentration upon one locale make a writer regional? That would mean that we judge the individual book by the relation of its locale to those of the author's other books, which is silly. Hemingway, then, would not be regional merely because he jumps around to a variety of settings, regardless of whether the individual books were written closely to a region. None of this makes sense.

It is interesting that no one classifies stories laid in the great cities of the world as regional. New York, London, Paris, for instance, are exempt. This is partly an old snobbery arising from the fact that early writers, beginning with the Romans, were urban, and even when their locale was out of town, as in Virgil and Shakespeare, they wrote for the people of their metropolis as being world opinion — and even today, for good criticism, we look to publications coming out of New York and Chicago.

The label "regional" is always put on writing that is placed in the sticks, or in the smaller cities. This limitation is plainly artificial, and one which sets up a classification which does not correspond to the qualities and characteristics of the writing itself. No one calls Sinclair Lewis regional. Why not? Because no one can avoid the national, and even wider, import of his writings even though so many are detailed studies of a single region.

We begin to reach a definition of the term, and one which emphatically excludes Faulkner. Regional writing, for the purposes of this discussion, is writing, regardless of the region in which it is placed, the interest of which does not transcend the interest of the region itself. If the word regional is to have any meaning at all, it must exclude writing that achieves universality.

Return to de Maupassant

LAST WEEK I was put up for several days in a club in Washington. In my bedroom were some bookshelves containing a handsomely printed edition of the complete works of Guy de Maupassant. Since fate determined that in the middle of the usual, hectic Washington rush I should have several grateful pools of idleness, I read in the volumes.

I had not read any de Maupassant since I was in college, when I found him disappointing. I didn't care for his stories, and they did not seem as spicy as they are advertised to be. I don't know how they got such a terrific reputation. Anyone looking for the salacious can beat the Frenchman's time any day for two bits at any soft-cover book counter. Vast numbers of youths, I imagine, over several generations, must have been disappointed when they dipped into the man's works — and at the same time, lured into reading some rather clever and smooth writing.

What this essay is about is de Maupassant's reputation as the founder of the short story. Since my early reading of him had been very slight, and at that time I was vague about what made a short story myself, I had always accepted that reputation without question. The hours I put in on him last week convince me that it is undeserved.

A short story is a definite form. Novels can be almost anything, they are allowed the loosest form, the greatest variety of forms, of any form of writing, but short stories, infinitely though they seem to vary from the virtual inaction and low pressure endings we find in *The New Yorker* to the too mechanically skillful, fast action, tightly plotted, strongly climaxed fiction of *The Saturday Evening Post*, remain a single, definite form. They are stories, not tales — that is, they have a plot, not mere incident or a sequence of incidents, an increase in intensity as they move on, a solution of one sort or another at the end.

Now, the first thing that de Maupassant's stories made me feel was that they reminded me of Grimm's fairy tales. The subject matter is, to put it mildly, different. De Maupassant deals largely with extra-marital love, which the fairy tales do not (at least as we know them), and he makes a good deal of use of tragic endings. Nonetheless, the structure of many of these, their lack of a true short story form, is reminiscent of Grimm's compilation. They may forecast the short story, as flint-tipped javelins forecast the bow and arrow, but that is all.

In them we do find a great use of the snapper ending that O. Henry later used so much, in fact did to death. We can find a number of elements that continued into the short story after that form had evolved. We also find that a lot of his shorter pieces should properly be classed as "sketches," that occur so often in the literary efforts of secondary school students. Again, of course, de Maupassant's subject matter is different. Any high school lad who wrote some of those compositions would be up before the principal in short order.

From where I sit, it looks as if Poe must stand as the real father of the short story as we now conceive of it. It is, then, originally an American form, and certainly some of its best practitioners have been American.

It may seem odd that, to typify de Maupassant's writing, I have compared it to two forms we associate with thorough innocence. Whether or not there is any real salaciousness in the man's work, his topics are certainly on the racy side. But his writing as a whole strikes me as naive. He is preoccupied with relationships that apparently he believes to be sophisticated or dashing, but are more often merely clumsy. His form is primitive. The end result of reading much of him is a sense of boredom, of "here we go again, and again, and again . . ."

The moral of all of which points to many present-day writers, who, like the Frenchman long ago, are getting by on exploiting the shock value of saying the supposedly unsayable. The shock value wears off. The end product is dull. It is the story that is good in itself that will always be read, the rest, no matter what the topic, becomes in the end like the sound of water running out of a tap.

The Ways of Words

"Areas," muttered the Man with the Calabash Pipe, "areas. If I hear any more of areas, I'll join one of those monasteries where they observe the vow of silence."

It is most unusual to find my learned friend mispronouncing a word, no matter how recondite, and now I thought I had him flat-footed. "What's the matter?" I asked. "Did someone lend you some bad records, or was your reception of last Saturday's opera bad? I thought most of the arias were fine." I gave the word "arias" the works.

He looked at me contemptuously. "I said 'areas.' I had reference to gobbledygook, to the ridiculous lingo affected by government employees and educators."

He set a match to his pipe, which had gone out, and leaned back in his armchair, puffing so furiously that the bowl soon glowed. There was only a pinch of tobacco left in the pipe, so that shortly he imbibed a red-hot blast. He jerked the pipe from his mouth and looked at it as one might at an old friend who has suddenly hit one with a brick, then he set it aside, selected his third-best, and filled it.

The incident and subsequent procedure of filling and lighting a fresh pipe calmed him.

"One of the great fallacies of would-be fine writers and talkers," he said, "is that it is more impressive, and generally better, to say a thing in three words instead of in one, and with an element of indirection rather than of bluntness. This vice is most highly developed among two groups — government people and educators.

"By educators I don't mean all who teach or otherwise deal in education, but the specialists, who have prepared themselves for teaching, not by becoming learned, which is the only true preparation, but by studying education." He paused, let smoke trickle from his mouth, and mentally contemplated the sinuosities of that last sentence.

"A year or two in any post-graduate department of education will unlearn just about anybody," he went on, "and it leads to that failing I now call 'area trouble.' "

He picked up a magazine and waved it sadly. "Here is an article by a top-flight educator. The man even makes sense, his grammar is excellent, his vocabulary betrays some study and reading outside of the science, or art, or hocus-pocus of education. But he can't help it. Listen."

He read: " 'What remedial procedures are indicated for the boy who consistently fails to make modal progress in the area of mathematics?' By 'area of mathematics' he means 'mathematics.' By the whole mess of verbiage he means, 'How do we help the boy who is poor in math?' "

He sighed. "Unhappily, 'help' has become 'remedial procedures.' The man not only talks like that, he thinks like that. He doesn't think 'mathematics,' he thinks 'area of . . .' He thinks something ill-defined, blurred at the edges. Probably, he can't find that the unfortunate kid is poor in math because he can't add, he has to plot a graph on him and determine how short he falls of 'modal progress' by means of quadratics and standard deviation."

He shook the magazine again. "Here he says, 'How far should we attempt to lead the student in this area at the secondary school level?' I would not subject even you to the language of his answer. The question, of course, means, 'How

much of this subject should be taught in secondary schools?'
But to his mind, 'at the secondary school level' sounds better.
Also, it keeps everything nice and vague."

"This has been around quite a while," I said, "why are you
suddenly so hot about it?"

"I've been reading applications for the Snickelfritz Scholar-
ships, and two out of three applicants, poor devils, try to make
themselves sound bright by using that kind of language. I
have deducted 10 per cent from my rating of every candidate
who uses the word 'area' in other than a geographical sense."

I was inclined to protest that that was unfair, but then I reflected that, before he sent in his ratings, he would unfailingly
restore those cuts. Ferocious on the surface, underneath my
friend is always tender toward men and mice alike.

I said, "I have to be going along. See you later." When I
was at the door, I said, "The dominant content of your subject matter indicates an above-modal affective response in the
area of literary stylistics, with especial reference to the use
of English at the adult level." Then I ducked out in a hurry.

The degradation of the meaning of words is one of the
means by which thinking is dulled. We think in words; if
words lose their meaning or become vague, or similar words
with quite different meanings, like uninterest and disinterest
or practicable and practical, are confused, our thinking is affected accordingly.

Since I am a writer, words are my tools even more than
they are most men's, but none of us can function without
them. I dislike the man who blunts, twists, or otherwise
spoils my tools. Nowadays there are some subjects that one
can hardly discuss usefully without taking half an hour first to
agree on the meaning of certain common words. All my objecting will probably do no good at all, but it helps me blow
off steam.

The October 12 number of *Time** carries a longish piece on the late H. W. Fowler and his *Modern English Usage.* The excuse for the piece was that the book has now sold well over half a million copies, but it seems to have been little more than an excuse. The *Time* boys, I suspect, just wanted to express their admiration for a great and unusual man.

That's an odd thing in itself, for, if Fowler had ever seen an example of the real *Time* style he probably would have been extremely caustic and thoroughly funny on the subject. He wrote his book to help protect good English usage, not as so many school-marms do, by trying to make their scholars obey arbitrary and unnatural rules, but by promoting clear thinking, unpretentious use of words, and a recognition that English is an evolving and changing language. He could not help expressing himself in unusual terms, with the result that what ought to be one of the driest books on earth is delightful and often hilarious reading.

One time my father and I got to discussing the phrase, "under the circumstances." Both of us agreed, since "circumstances" means "what is standing around," that the usual phrase was incorrect and one should say "in the circumstances." Then my father suggested that we look it up in Fowler, so I found the passage and read aloud, in a clear voice:

"The objection to 'under the circumstances' and insistence that 'in the circumstances' is the only right form, because what is round us is not over us, is puerile. To point out that 'round' applies as much to vertical as to horizontal relations, and that a threatening sky is a circumstance no less than a threatening bulldog . . . might lay one open to the suspicion of answering fools according to their folly. A more polite reply is that 'the circumstances' means the state of affairs, and

* 1953.

may naturally be conceived as exercising the pressure under which one acts. . . ."

My father grunted when I read "fools according to their folly"; by the time I finished the passage we were thoroughly crushed, but also we were laughing. It is that kind of book; it is the only book I know of that makes good English fun.

I'd like to see it in the hands of, and read, marked, learned, and inwardly digested, by every English teacher in the land. Whoever uses Fowler will have no fear of splitting an infinitive or ending a sentence with a preposition when those practices make the better, clearer, more graceful statement. They will be cured of such illiteracies as "more unique," and at least less inclined to use a long and ill-fitting word under the delusion that it is more elegant than a shorter, precise one.

Different languages work in vastly different ways, and grow differently. English, like all the Indo-European languages, is deeply concerned with time. It is almost impossible to make a sentence that does not express the idea of past, present, or future. Our daily thinking, our mathematics, even our nuclear physics, are all conditioned by this concern with time, and the point of view towards it that is built into our daily speech.

So vigorous a language as Navaho is also growing and increasing its capabilities, but it is little concerned with time. Tense is less developed. Navaho, however, pays detailed attention to the nature of an action. We say "I throw," meaning any one of a series of actions that causes any object, or several objects, to move through the air. To us, it's all throwing.

Navaho finds that inadequate. Throwing a rope is not the same as throwing a ball, and both those actions are different from throwing a handful of gravel. The verb reflects these differences. To us, Navaho seems under-developed in regard to time; to a Navaho, English is sadly inaccurate in regard to the nature of an action.

There are languages that disregard past, present, and future almost entirely, but require a speaker to use grammatical forms that show whether the statement he happens to be making is something he knows from his own observation, or something he has been told. The speakers of such a language might well wonder how we could advance as far as we have in science when we fail to distinguish between hearsay and first-hand knowledge.

Languages also grow in different ways. English is exceptionally hospitable to new words, both home-made inventions, such as "jeep," and words from other languages such as "wigwam" or "corral." Much of the larger part of our vocabularies, even in ordinary, daily speech, is made up of words borrowed from other languages, yet English is so vigorous that it has absorbed this mass without ceasing to be itself.

German, which at one time was fairly hospitable to foreign words, underwent a conscious change. German intellectuals started a program of replacing borrowed words with compounds of their own tongue. So it is that in books written a hundred years ago you find such easily recognized words as "ethnologie," then a generation later they are replaced by new compounds, in that case "voelkerkunde." German does not seem to have gained anything by this shift.

Navaho growth is somewhat on the German order. Navaho interpreters take pride in not using borrowed words to express even the newest, most difficult ideas. A monthly newspaper is published in Navaho which deals with a wide range of matters, including items of world news, pending legislation, new regulations, and so forth. It is astonishing to see how very few English words appear in the text. Certainly not over a dozen are in common use.

This drive to maintain pure Navaho is understandable. They are a small, proud nation trying to maintain their integrity in the middle of a very large one. Strengthening and expanding the mother tongue is one means to this end.

The speech of the various Apache tribes is closely related to Navaho, but they have not developed this urge. Their languages have changed but little from the limited vocabulary that served their needs before they were faced by our complex world. They have to fall back on English to deal with the new things, with the result that some of their tribal councils now transact much of their business entirely in English. The news-letter published by the San Carlos Apaches is written in English, although Apache could be written, and printed, with the alphabet the Navahos use. The present trend in the Apache languages is to dwindle and grow weaker.

Each language moves its own way, and in each you can read a good deal of the history and character of the people. The general direction of our own tongue is toward ever simpler grammar and an ever larger number of available words. There is probably no one person living who is able to use all the words that are now recognized as good English. This process is enlivened by the constant development of new slang, which makes daily English more fun than most speech. From a writer's point of view, you can't beat it.

Discouraging as it may be to know that the publishers of Merriam's version of Noah Webster's dictionary have sold out to those curious theorists who hold that anything people say is equally good English, regardless, it is a healthy sign that the storm the new edition has created, which has been raging for some months now in periodicals of all sorts, popular and technical, has finally become news. An interest in the English language, American version, is not confined to a select few.

The new Merriam edition is portentously called "Webster's Third New International Dictionary of the English Language." I hope everyone knows that Noah Webster has been long dead, his copyright lapsed ages ago, and any publisher who so desires can use the name Webster.

As for "International" in there, it's for the birds. This dictionary embraces as sound, permanent English every bit of transient American slang, every nonce-word, every passing affectation of the decade, without any distinction between such words and those new ones that have in fact become incorporated into standard English, so that the writer or speaker who lets himself be guided by the new book will speak a dialect intelligible only in this country, and not to everyone even here.

English has become the nearest thing we now have to an international language. There are things like Esperanto, a number of them, but they have never taken hold. More people today speak English than any other tongue, which puts us in a fortunate position — provided we continue to know how to speak and understand English ourselves.

Whether we can manage that is a question. We seem to have fallen into a habit of speech that could be called "approximate English," or "near-miss English." For instance, the words "disinterest" and "uninterest" look similar. Their correct meanings are not at all similar, but it is common practice now to use "disinterest" to mean "uninterest." What word such a user will employ when he wants to say "disinterest," I know not. Perhaps the concept is too lofty for him to have any occasion to express it.

All around you can see similar examples of words being used instead of other words the sounds of which they approximate. A recent development that, I note, is gaining some currency among anthropologists, is "predominate" for "predominant." That is a type of confusion that the non-phonic, look-and-say method of teaching reading (not followed, fortunately, in the Santa Fe schools) could produce.

In the same number of this paper that carried the dictionary story, we read that the city council meeting "dispensed with its business under the eyes of a uniformed police officer. . . ." As a howler, that's a beaut, with its amusing suggestion of a Nazi-style take-over. We know what the writer meant, which was not what he said. He fell victim, I suspect, to the fallacy that a long word is better than a short one. "Did its business" says what he meant, and is perfectly safe.

We don't only confuse and louse up words, but proverbial sayings are going to pot. I have heard an astonishing number of people recently speak of "putting your John Henry" on something, as, autographing a book. What a pity. John Henry is, I believe, a mythical Negro character of Paul Bunyanesque qualities. He has nothing to do with signing one's name. Every school-child, you would think, would know that the first man to step up and sign his name to the Declaration of Independence, thereby automatically putting himself on the King's list of traitors to be hanged if caught, was John Hancock, and that he signed his name in a very clear, round hand. For that reason, and a very good one it is, in this country John Hancock has been a synonym for "signature" for a hundred and seventy-odd years.

Near-miss English makes it possible for me to say that since I am disinterested in the predominate opinion I will not put my John Henry on the rather unique document you offer me — and a distressing number of people will see nothing wrong with the statement.

As a professional writer who, however limited his abilities, nonetheless loves the art, the slow decay of the English language is to me a constant source of sorrow. Good English, correct, standard English, sharp and definite in meanings, vast in range, infinitely varied in vocabulary, capable of the most remarkable phonic manipulations, is a writer's dream language. I do not think there is any other that so lends itself to writers' varied purposes.

Wherefore it is to me a cause of sadness as I see it being blurred or weakened with sloppy, Merriam-Webster permissiveness and simple confusions.

We are suffering also from a curious prissiness, a fear of using certain excellent and old-established words, that seems to me quite pointless. What, for instance, has happened to Asia Minor? You almost never hear it mentioned any more. And what have we gained by that absurd term — a British concoction, I believe — Middle East? The Middle East is not in the middle and most of it is not the east. Asia Minor means something, and so does North Africa. Why the change?

And, speaking of Asia, what happened, a decade or so ago, to that fine and universally accepted old adjective, Asiatic? Why all of a sudden has everyone taken to saying Asian, as if they were afraid their dentures would come loose? George Washington's dentures fitted badly, but he said "Asiatic," and a good, sound, strong old word it is. Why this Asian elegance?

Also, so far as I know, no one feels that there is anything out of line about calling a native of England an Englishman, of France a Frenchman, or of Scotland a Scotchman. And yet, also in recent decades, a curious convention has grown up that one must not say "Chinaman." The done thing nowadays is "a Chinese." Just like, "a Japanese."

Of course, "Chinawoman" never did get into the vocabulary, and, as we all remember, Madame Chiang was not only charming but very forceful. Perhaps she set this change up with Franklin D. Roosevelt. Perhaps it was ratified at Yalta as part of the big deal to undermine the United States Constitution, and that's the real reason why John Birch got himself shot. The possibilities are most intriguing.

Another good, solid, useful word that has gone by the board is Negress. This was entirely accepted when I was a boy, along with poetess, sculptress, and actress. Of them all, only actress seems to remain current, the others having fallen prey to a levelling and aimless extension of feminism. There is, to my mind, as much difference between a Negro and a Negress as there is between a Frenchman and a Frenchwoman, and any native of France will be glad to tell you how considerable that difference is. This disappearance of these feminine forms is a loss of quality from the language.

When I was a boy, we occasionally partook of a rare, tropical comestible, a vegetable that went by the strong, descriptive name of alligator pear. It is one of Madison Avenue's minor but dismaying triumphs that it has been able to replace that term by the pseudo-Spanish invention, "avocado," thus progressing one little step further in the endless campaign to grind and dilute the English language into the bland linguistic equivalent of an ulcer diet.

The book, *From Here to Eternity*, has unloosed a new furore over the question of using or not using four-letter words. *Life* even ran an editorial on it. It brings up a writing problem about which I have never yet been able to make up my mind.

English is the only language which expresses almost all ideas on a series of different levels. The ideas expressed by the four-letter words can be expressed by a series of euphemisms and periphrases, by other words of a more acceptable nature, and finally, with an effect of extreme crudity, by what were originally our basic terms.

It is interesting that Shakespeare, who wrote broadly and frankly, and who, as in the opening scene of *Othello*, was not in the least afraid of being coarse, never saw fit to use these words. Yet he can most certainly handle realistic and convincing dialogue.

In a relatively simple language such as Navaho, each of these concepts can be expressed only by one simple, direct word.

A Navaho uses those words relatively freely, because he has no others. When Walter Dyk published that moving Navaho autobiography, *Son of Old Man Hat,* he chose to translate the Navaho terms by the English four-letter words. Because of the very different place that these words occupy in English, he gave the narrative an effect of mere coarseness, almost bestiality, which was undoubtedly absent from the mind and speech of the Navaho narrator.

The curious foulness of mouth of "single men in barracks" is notorious. They do not so much swear, as lard their talk with filth. It has been suggested that this is an unconscious psychological expression of their deprivations. Perhaps so.

At any rate, it is clear to anyone who has listened to them that they do not themselves hear what they are saying. In the South Pacific, I remember a middle-aged master sergeant who told me wistfully of his desire to get back to his (obscenity) home, and his (obscenity) wife, and who then showed me a photograph of his wife and of his (obscenity) pretty little (obscenity) daughter.

If I had been fool enough to have made any crack deriving from the meaning of his obscenities, he would have undoubtedly shoved my teeth through the back of my neck, rank or no rank. In other words, he did not hear himself.

What happens, then, when a writer renders these expressions exactly in printed dialogue? Do they have the same value then as they had spoken into the absorptive air, among similar-speaking men? I seriously wonder. Speech is not the same as written language. The dialogue of such masters of "natural" conversation as Hemingway and Wister still lies within a convention, more orderly, less rambling, more to their purpose, than was ever natural speech. So was Ring Lardner's.

Writing is done within definite conventions, just as the theater is. Then, does not exact reproduction of conversation

serve its purpose? Is there, in fact, ever any exact reproduction of conversation outside of the work of a court reporter?
I doubt it. The most realistic reproduction of conversation is
still an artifice. The exact reproduction, then, of the obscenities which are in fact a part of the conversation of certain people becomes a question, not of exactitude of reporting, but of
the impact of that reproduction upon a reader who is not
himself living in that milieu.

I cease at this point to be competent to reach a decision,
because of my dislike of that kind of talk anyhow. I don't
know how it affects others. What I do know is that it is a
writer's business to convey truths more important than meet
the ordinary eye, by selection, enlargement of what he wants
to emphasize, arrangement, and alteration of scale. It is
within that frame that we must place the "exact" renderings
of speech, to determine in the end, not whether the given
sentence is exact, but whether it conveys to the ordinary
reader the impact, the effect, the revelation of the speaker,
which are so much truer and so much more important than
the speech itself.

Books and Children

B EING A PERSON who becomes furious if anyone interrupts his studies, his meditations, or his occasional literary efforts, the Man with the Calabash Pipe is occasionally and paradoxically addicted to dropping in upon others when at work. I was at my typewriter, trying to dream up something, when he came sloping into the room, and as usual, began by looking over the books on the table in a censorious manner.

He removed his pipe — his largest calabash — from between his lips, blew a cloud of smoke at me, and said, "Rereading *David Copperfield*, eh? How do you like it now you're grown up?"

"Parts of it are grand," I said, "like the Dotheboys' Hall section, but take it by and large, I couldn't stick it."

"I'm not surprised." He paused, then added, with an evil gleam in his eyes, "It's not the Heep, it's the humility."

I would have thrown the ashtray at him, but in laughing at his own atrocity he blew sparks and ashes all over himself and was further punished by a violent fit of coughing.

When he had straightened out I fingered the keys of my typewriter suggestively, and then asked, remembering, "Weren't you going to Albuquerque today?"

"That had been my plan, to borrow a copy of *Novum Organum* from the University library. Unfortunately, my car wouldn't start."

"Small wonder, that jalopy."

"The little car's all right," he said, in the tone of a mother
defending a dearly loved but slightly idiot child. "It's just
that when I was hosing it down, I must have got some water
in the carburetor."

Quick as a flash I put in, "I see. It's not the heap, it's the
humidity."

For a moment he looked at me with the expression of a
wounded gazelle, then his eyes cleared and a half-smile appeared upon his lips. He knocked out of his pipe, vaguely in
the direction of my hearthstone, the unattractive remnants of
shag in the bottom of it, reached for my humidor, and said,
"Mind if I borrow some of your weed?"

I constrained myself to a reluctant silence of consent. He
shoved about an ounce of expensive mixture into his stove,
took up a handful of my matches, and set about lighting it.
Between flames and puffs, he meditated aloud.

"Why do we speak of 'borrowing' tobacco? One gives and
receives it, like food, and like food, it is often part of the ritual of hospitality. In the end, among friends everyone comes
out even, and richer by the warmth of mutual giving — a
system highly ritualized among the Hopis, but not badly
worked out among ourselves."

All very well, I thought, except that having him use up
one's tobacco is like being taken for a steak dinner by a man
who habitually dines on earthworms and lean, ground shoe-
leather.

His eye lit on *David Copperfield* again. "That," he said, "is
a school-marm's classic. That is, They, whoever They are,
have said it is one, and hence it is forced down children's
throats according to an educational system guaranteed to destroy the reading habit. Classics are not those works that have
been so denominated by an anonymous, oligarchical election,"
he paused to savor those last words, "they are those that are

new and delightful to each generation. At its best, *David Cop-perfield* is a classic, all right, at its worst, nauseating. Forcing it on the young is like trying to inculcate a taste in oysters by alternately offering good and bad ones. It takes a great writer to be really bad; *vide* the Catalogue of Ships."

He put another match to his pipe. "Am I keeping you from work?"

"You are," I said, with emphasis.

"Hmmm — your Sunday column, I suppose. Nine hundred words a week. That ought to be simple, and an excellent discipline for you."

"It's not simple at all," I told him. "Here it's almost the deadline, it's spring outside, the irises are blooming, the editor will wither me with a glance if I'm late again, and I haven't an idea in my head."

He walked to the door. "Well, I'll leave you to your task. Take comfort, nature abhors a vacuum." He turned and looked at me benevolently. "With you, my friend, it isn't the heat, it's the stupidity."

He vanished behind a smokescreen of his own making.

My young son recently received his first book, contemplation of which renews a number of thoughts concerning that branch of literature known as "juveniles."

For nearly a generation, now, the child experts and psychologists have been preaching that we must not talk baby-talk to little children. Teach them straight English to start with, they urge, so that they don't have to learn twice. Baby-talk is a real temptation to the adult, it is part of a whole complex of methods of revelling in one's child, or in little children in general. Most of us, doing as we are told, resist this temptation, with the gratifying outcome that each child goes through a stage of creating its own baby-talk, with wonderful results.

The publishers of juvenile books make a great to-do about

child psychology. They allege that each book is carefully ad-
justed to conform to the latest and best theories, and that
their publications cause benefits far beyond mere entertain-
ment. And yet, a brief survey of juveniles during my own life-
time shows that they are tending more and more towards
baby-talk, especially in the illustrations.

When I was a child, my *Mother Goose* had illustrations
that an adult could enjoy. To a child they were fascinating.
Old Mother Hubbard was a well-drawn, wrinkled old woman,
The Old Woman Who Lived in a Shoe was also realistic, old,
and harassed. In the Oz books, Glinda the Good, to take one
example, was a grown-up and truly queenly woman. These
illustrations, which lived up to the text, were supremely satisfactory.

Now the Oz books have been re-illustrated. Glinda the
Good appears as a child dressed up in her mother's clothes.
She has been reduced to baby-talk. In my son's *Mother
Goose*, Old Mother Hubbard is a chubby little girl with spec-
tacles on; again, a little girl playing grownup. The rest of the
illustrations are similar. They have been remorselessly simpli-
fied, and reduced to the absolute nadir of draughtsmanship.

Children's imaginations can take them in the most unexpected directions. If they want to play grownup, they do not
imagine themselves simply as children in adult clothing.
When they read about an old woman, they have a right to imagine, and to expect to see, a picture of an old woman. When
they read about a queen who is also a beneficent witch, they
have a right to be shown a picture of a benign, queenly
woman.

The "juvenile" business is a good deal of a racket. Since
there is a whole new audience of children in any age-group
every couple of years, there is really no reason why floods of
new juveniles should be published annually. They are not

aimed at the children, but at the parents. The horrid, new, cute illustrations of the Oz books, the baby-doll pictures in my son's *Mother Goose*, are aimed at the parents' secret love of baby-talk.

The sales method is the same as that by which a bachelor can be fooled into spending a lot of money to buy a baby a crystal porringer (I am not inventing). It is the same trick we see in the perfectly awful neckties that even so sedate a store as Brooks Brothers displays at Christmas, to lure the women gift-shoppers. The parents are made happy, while the unfortunate child is subjected to bad art, as often as not mated with equally bad literature.

What we set before our children's eyes and what we pour into their minds is just as important as what we put in their mouths. Juvenile books should be the most carefully screened and the most choosily selected of all forms of publication. Instead they are a deluge of almost anything that anyone thinks can be sold.

Having long held a highly dubious opinion of the whole business of writing and publishing juveniles, it is with mixed feelings that I read the announcement of a forthcoming juvenile of my own in a publisher's catalogue.* No author can properly judge his own work; only indirectly by reflection from reviewers (who must always be taken with a discount), acquaintances (usually much too kind), and chance remarks, may I finally form some idea whether I have avoided the very vices I so dislike.

Certainly, the sales of this book will be no test. The juvenile business, one might almost say the juvenile racket, exists for sales. It frequently achieves them, and, as in the case of books for adults, popularity is as yet no proof of quality. At least, that goes for immediate popularity. There is the long-

* *Cochise of Arizona.*

term popularity, enjoyed alike by *Hamlet* and *Peter Rabbit*, that is, I think, proof. The author, unfortunately, does not last long enough to learn of it.

The publishers, when they engaged me to write this book, sent me others they were proudly bringing out, to give me an idea of how the thing is done. They stressed two things to me: That I should stick to a simple, Anglo-Saxon, subject-predicate-object sentence structure, and that the ideas presented should be equally simple.

The books they gave me to read only confirmed the impression I had so long had — that the great majority of juveniles are written by people to whom writing is merely business, and who have neither artistic gift nor the true writer's conscience. In what were supposed to be educative works, accurately true to life, I found not only wooden, stock characters and character behaviors that were basically untrue, but also such gross impossibilities as a boy who rode his horse a hundred miles in one day, with two hours out for lunch. The ideas and the style were certainly simple, the stories maintained constant action, and no doubt the youths who read them will like them. I still find the business on the disreputable side.

There is a challenge in juvenile writing for writers who take their profession proudly as an art. One is required to be simple in style, statement, and vocabulary, but this does not mean that one may not try to write beautifully and even passionately. It is possible, within these limits, to achieve fine writing, to offer the reader an artistic experience. To do so, for children in the process of forming their taste, should be one of the writer's principal aims.

Further, that business about simple ideas is false. Children think. Children, by the time they are around ten, are thinking about extremely complex things. A book worthy of being put in their hands is not one that contains nothing to stretch their active minds, but rather one that has accepted and won the challenge of presenting tough ideas in simple, clear terms.

Each of these last two paragraphs contains the word "challenge." The word is frequently abused, but it is still valid. All writing, every undertaking in the arts, should be a response to challenge, although much of it (mea culpa) is not. When it comes to writing for children, the sense of being challenged, the sense of artistic responsibility, should be especially great.

All of which, written in connection with a forthcoming juvenile of my own, sounds as smug as one of those numbered pieces by my old friend, Dr. Crane. I am not feeling smug. I seriously doubt that I have been able to meet my own standards, and one reason for writing this particular piece at this particular time is to get it off before anyone can throw my own book at me in refutation. It is, as it were, a confession before the act.

One curious thing is that the juvenile editors themselves are cowards. Rather than seeking to give children the best and the most unusual, they try to press their writers down to the mediocre and the usual. It happens that the particular thing I wrote made no sense without something being said about the nonanthropomorphic concept of God. Interpreting those last four words into language for ten-year-olds was definitely a challenge. That I tried it frightened the editors still. I refused to delete it, and now they are delighted with it. Now, with real nervousness, they and I await the test of whether the real-life ten-year-olds will accept it.

The writer for adults sends his work into a tough market and takes his chances. The writer for children essentially does the same, but his story will be read by uncritical minds, the plausibly bad will be accepted as readily as the good, and it is that which should keep him humble and a little frightened.

If You Must Write

IN ADVISING young writers, anyone who knows what he is about stresses the importance of avoiding "literary language." Literary language seems to be something with which the young are infected by teachers who don't know their business. It consists of two elements.

The first of these is an attempt to imitate the style of classics written in past centuries. Even in the past fifty years our written and spoken modes of expression have changed importantly. In this country, with Hemingway as perhaps the strongest single influence, writing has tended to return to the vigorous, simple style of Tudor times before the influence of Euphues, a style which exploits to the fullest the best qualities of the English language. This, of course, is not an imitative return but an intuitive evolution. Any attempt to imitate a past mode results in awkward, artificial writing.

The second element is injection into the literary product of the longest, most impressive words, imbedded in the longest, most complex sentences, of which the writer is capable. This is also the vice of bad oratory. The results are usually laughable. We should not find this vice had we not teachers who think that polysyllables and periodic sentences are more elegant than short words and the Anglo-Saxon construction. The other would not exist if there were not teachers who feel that any deviation from the style of their favorite, dead authors was improper.

Good writing in any age has been natural to that age. It has always more or less approximated the manner of speech of that age. I say "approximated." Written language is not the same as spoken language and in the nature of things cannot be.

Written words dwell before our eyes. We hear them, are conscious of the phonetic beauty of good writing, through a transposition from one sense to another performed within our brains. Our apperception of writing is more complex and takes longer than of speech. Writing also lacks the aids of tone of voice, facial expression, and gesture. From these differences inevitably arise differences in the two uses of language. The spoken word, instantly evanescent, must use various devices to drive home the important point; the written must use other devices to make up for the lack of the voice's emphasis.

The best place to see what happens to the pure spoken word when it is put into writing unchanged is in the reports of hearings of the committees of Congress. In these we get, verbatim, the wording of unrehearsed exchanges. We find, even in the speech of highly educated men long accustomed to public debate, curiously vaguely constructed sentences. We find a constant repetition of a single, key word, a repetition which mortally offends the ear when we see it written, but which we should not notice were we listening.

In the course of my anthropological work I have dealt at some length with storytellers, pre-literate artists of language, men who had reputations in their tribes not unlike the repute of a writer with us. With these men I found I had a good deal in common. We all had an ear for a good phrase, for the exceptionally apt word. We all responded equally to a story-idea with interesting possibilities. But, from that point I thought in terms of what I could write, they in terms of what they could tell, which means, among other things, what they could enact. These men were half litterateurs, half actors. They made full, untranscribable use of pantomime.

The primitive storyteller of note has a wider range of gifts than are required of a writer. That does not mean that he would make a good writer. Among educated people, we all know plenty of whom people say, "If only he would write down the stories he tells." He doesn't, because he can't. Different channels of the brain are involved. It is possible so to injure the brain as to render speech impossible without interfering with the ability to write, and vice versa. It is not surprising then that, conversely to the type mentioned above, so many writers read aloud extremely badly.

Writing and speaking are two different uses of language. Good writing can never be identical with speech. This applies even to dialogue. Even in the work of such a master of dialogue as Hemingway, his naturalistic talk is still better arranged, better constructed, freer of repetitions than is the case in nature. Good writing, however, eternally approaches speech; it is of its time, it is never "literary."

III

Indians in the Southwest

The American Indian:
Falsehoods and Truths

THE EASE WITH which we forget our past and replace the true traditions with myths continues to surprise me. A highly false mythology has grown up about the art school movement at the Santa Fe Indian School in the 1930's and has spread widely. Its latest manifestation was in a column of a few months ago by Dr. Harry Wood, art critic for *The Arizona Republic*, a Phoenix paper.

In his column Dr. Wood repeated the false story that Indian students were gathered in Santa Fe and there taught to imitate Persian paintings, so that a highly artificial, unnatural school of pseudo-Indian paintings resulted. Nothing could be further from the truth.

Modern Southwestern Indian painting began around 1918, when local anthropologists encouraged Pueblo Indians to make pictures of dances that, it was believed, were about to be lost forever. From this simple endeavor rapidly developed a whole school that caught the astonished attention of artists. About that time, a number of Kiowas began turning out pictures, under the auspices of the University of Oklahoma. The Kiowas had behind them the Plains tradition of realistic painting, which had not existed in the Southwest.

The earliest documented observation that Pueblo painting resembled Persian (and Indian) art was made by Amanda Coomaraswamy in 1920. Later observers saw resemblances rather to the work of Chinese and Japanese painters, but no one who was around at the time was ever under the delusion that these resemblances were the result of influences of any kind. To my mind, the resemblances were never strong.

In the 1920's, Indian schools still taught children to copy outdated European and white American work. There was a print of horses by Rosa Bonheur, of which I used to see scores of copies. Against this trend Santa Fe's Indian Arts Fund set itself. The Exposition of American Indian Tribal Art became a national sensation. The Misses Martha and Elizabeth White had a large part in setting that up.

Out of these developments, plus the dedication of Miss Dorothy Dunn and the wisdom of Olive Rush, who insisted that Indians, not herself, decorate the new Indian School dining room, came the establishment of an art school under Miss Dunn, at the Indian School.

None of the people then concerned with the promotion of Indian arts and crafts believed in telling Indians what to do. They all saw that, if anything was to come of it, the Indians must move into new developments of their own, be it adapting k'etohs to make covers for cigarette boxes or painting large water colors that could and did win honors in open competition in Paris.

(And incidentally, the first adaptation of Pueblo women's costumes for modern wear, such as were featured recently in this paper, was done here by Alice Evans in the 1930's.)

After World War II both the art and the crafts schools were pretty deliberately killed off. By then the former had stimulated, not only a Pueblo movement, but a Plains and a Navaho-Apache one, each different from the others, each rooted in the past, moving towards the future. Many of the artists fell away into illustrationy commercialism, especially those who came under the influence of the Oklahoman, Acee Blue Eagle. One group here worked on the assembly-line system, lin-

The American Indian: Falsehoods and Truths 137

ing up a series of drawings, then one man putting in one color along the line, another the next, and so on.

There are still a few good artists whose work is firmly based on their Indian heritage, however far they may have gone beyond it. Given the wonderful outburst that was stimulated by the Santa Fe School, we can say with certainty that there should be many more. That is one of the challenges confronting the new Institute of American Indian Arts here.

Now that Santa Fe is in the season of many visitors, it seems appropriate to answer some of the many wild superstitions about Indians, not only among Easterners, but among a great many of our permanent residents. The notes below are in essence answers to questions — or, often enough, dogmatic statements — encountered in the past year.

1. Indians are citizens and they have the right to vote. Charles Curtis, vice president of the United States, was an Indian, with the same status as any Indian you see when you visit a pueblo.

2. Indians can leave their reservations whenever they please, go where they wish, live where they choose, and engage in any business they think they are competent to handle.

3. Indians do not receive a pension from the government. They have to earn their own livings. If they do well enough, they must pay income tax like anybody else.

4. It is not true that, if you give an Indian a lift and he is hurt in an accident while in your car, the federal government will sue you. If the accident occurs on Indian land, and the Indian is smart and mean enough to sue, the action will come up in federal court; otherwise the state court. Mr. Indian in either case will have to find and pay his own attorney, just like anyone else.

5. Indians are not oil-rich. Out of some 450,000 of them, about 3,000 have individual incomes from oil, and most of

these have less than $2,500 a year. Some tribes have income from oil, gas, mines, and so forth, such as the Navahos and Jicarilla Apaches in this vicinity. If their annual take were divided among all members of the tribe, there would hardly be enough for one good meal per person. The tribes use income of this kind for public purposes of various sorts, such as drought relief, pay of tribal police, and hiring business advisers.

6. Pueblo Indians do not have to get permission from the governor of their pueblo before having a baby.

7. The word pueblo is pronounced "pwayblow" and not "pee-eeblow," or "pew-eeblow" or "MacGarnigle."

8. The word Apache is pronounced "Apatchee." The French "apaches" took their name from the American tribe and Gallicized the word. Referring to those tribes as "Apash" may be intended to show off the speaker's profound dunking in French cultuah; what it does is show off the speaker's ignorance (sometimes pronounced "igger-ance").

9. The word Navaho — oh well, let's don't go into that.

10. The dancers who take part in ceremonies at the various pueblos do so without pay. They dance because they believe in the ceremonies, and because they are proud of their traditions and their art. If, on the side, the community can make a little money out of letting you take pictures, that is to the public good. Minor dances are also performed commercially, such as the dances at Tesuque for the American Express tours. Sometimes such dances are authentic, sometimes they are not.

11. The money you pay when you visit Taos Pueblo does not mean that Taos is "degenerate" or "commercialized." Having been plagued by visitors for years, the Indians had sense enough to cash in on the plague. The money is scrupulously accounted for and used for civic purposes.

12. Your behavior in the presence of Indians, loud or quiet, rude or polite, prying or considerate, will govern their opinion of you exactly as when you are in the presence of other Americans.

One of the astonishing things about New Mexico is what people who even live here do not know about Indian matters. A case in point is the current furore over the claim of the Taos Indians, now pending before the Indian Claims Commission.

This claim was entered eight years ago, pursuant to the Indian Claims Act, the purpose of which is to clear away once and for all the many Indian claims, valid and not valid, against the government. Taos Pueblo claims damages for the taking of portions of the Taos Indian Grant by non-Indians and for the taking of certain other lands; it also claims ownership of the watershed of the Rio Pueblo de Taos east and north of the grant. In the latter case, the Indians want the land, not money. Whether they can get it or not remains to be seen.

The watershed includes the sacred area around the Blue Lake, which is the Indians' most holy temple, and certain other sacred shrines. Hence the Indian feeling about it is strong.

Neither the Spanish nor the Mexican governments interfered with the Taos Indians' immemorial use and occupancy of this area, nor did the U.S. until this century.

In 1904 the Chief of the Bureau of Biological Survey persuaded the Indians that inclusion of the watershed in the new National Forest system would be the means of protecting it forever for Taos use. The Indians agreed, the land was included in the Carson National Forest, and for some years was kept exclusively for the tribe.

In 1909 the Forest Service renewed its assurance of protec-

tion of the Taos interests, in writing. In 1918 the supervisor of
the Carson Forest wrote to the governor of Taos, restating that
the watershed was for exclusive Indian use, and asking his
permission to allow some non-Indian cattle to graze on a part
of it. It would be hard to find a solider admission of the Taos
basic title.

In 1930, an attorney for the Pueblo Lands Board persuaded Taos Pueblo to give up their claims to thousands of
dollars for the parts of the grant they had lost, promising that
in exchange they could get the Rio Pueblo watershed. The
Indians were so pleased that they gave the attorney fifty dollars. He had no authority to make any such promises, and all
the Indians ever got was a partial, exclusive-use right under an
Act of Congress passed in 1933.

Meantime, the old promises and agreements were forgotten, as usual with white men, and more and more non-Indians
were being allowed in the Blue Lake area. This was a great
grief to the Indians. They felt, and feel, betrayed, and in my
judgment they are right.

Now, Taos Pueblo is not, as reported, trying to recapture
the village of Taos or any part of it. They may have some
damages coming to them from the federal government; that
is all. They are trying to recapture the watershed. The first
step in regard to that will be the actual trial of their claim.
The Indian Claims Commission cannot give land. It can
only find that the Indians did or did not own the land aborig-
inally and then say how much money loss the Indians have
suffered.

When the Claims Commission has made its finding, it will
be time for Taos Pueblo to decide what to do next. If the
finding is in their favor, we may cherish a faint hope that the
white men will act with justice and a little generosity.

As noted, this case has been pending for eight years. So

far, a date for the actual hearing has not even been set. Naturally, the Indians are impatient.

There is no question of "giving" an area of land to Taos Pueblo. The question is of restoring to the Pueblo land that belongs to it and that was taken from it by false promises. If the Indian Claims Commission finds that in fact the land does, or did, belong to the tribe, then restoring it to the tribe becomes a matter of simple justice.

Hopis and Navahos

THIS WONDERFUL RAIN (some of which we got in an exces-
sively concentrated form last Wednesday) has been reaching all the way from here to beyond the Hopi country in
Arizona. I was over there last week, and all the way along
there were rainstorms and rainbows, and water standing in
the fields. It was a really wonderful thing to see the change
in the look of the country between last Sunday, when we
headed west, and Thursday evening when we got back.

Grass is coming up all over. Regardless of the damage the
cloudburst may have done in Santa Fe, wet weather like this
is a gift of millions of dollars to the people of the Southwest.

Over in the Hopi villages, this is the time when the Kachinas, the divine intermediaries between man and God, go
home. They have been in the villages, invisible presences,
since December; now they return to their own place. It is a
time of intense and beautiful ritual.

During the time that the Kachinas are present, they are
impersonated in the masked dances. There is more than im-
personation, the spirit of the Kachina is present in the mask,
which is sacred. That is why Indians are so profoundly upset when obtuse white men, regarding a mask merely as a curiosity, misuse it.

The home-going of these divine beings is marked by an especially fine masked dance. To see this being carried out, in
the happiness of water on the fields after so terribly long a

time of drought, under a sky made dramatic by rain-promising clouds, is an experience to remember. The rain makes rough camping. It makes the crude, dirt tracks that pass for roads in that country horrifying to drive over. Nonetheless, the trip was more than worthwhile.

Also, the Navaho Tribal Council was in session. At the same time we had our cloudburst, they had one at Window Rock. It got going just as the chairman called a recess in mid-morning, when the delegates get a coffee break. They were stranded in the Council House with a sudden, new river between them and their coffee.

The Navaho Tribal Council is a genuine governing body. Its proceedings are dignified and effective. There is nothing naive about the thinking revealed in their debates, and they scrutinize the wording of the resolutions offered with care. One does encounter evidences of ignorance and misinformation, and naturally, those delegates who do not even speak English find some technical matters difficult to understand.

After spending a few hours listening to them, you are left with a strong feeling of the great potential of this tribe. If they can manage their affairs as effectively as they do, when half of their population has never been to school, what will they be like when — and if — we ever make it possible for them to raise a whole generation that can read and write? The criminal thing is that we have not yet made it possible for more than half of their youngsters to get into a school, and heaven only knows when we are going to give them the same opportunities we give all other citizens.

So long as they remain as they are now, they remain a people who cannot fend for themselves, a people who must be helped and protected. It will cost a lot of money to get every Navaho child of school age into school; it will cost a lot more to do all we must do to enable the Navahos, and many other tribes, to face the world on equal terms with the rest of us, ready and able to fend for themselves, but whenever we make up our minds to spend those amounts, we shall make one of the best investments we have ever made.

All in all, I had a grand trip. I saw the two principal aspects of the Southwestern Indian of today — the ancient ceremony conducted in deep faith and in solemn beauty, and the modern governing body coming to grips with the innumerable problems of the outside world. Both were inspiring, and over all, from west to east, was the blessing of the rain.

Horned Husband Kachina Chief
Returns

MY OLD FRIEND, the Horned Husband Kachina Chief from Awatovi, took a pinch of my pipe tobacco and rolled it in a cornhusk. As I have told before, he speaks no English, and I no Hopi, so we converse in Navaho, a language neither of us could exactly be said to command. To the best of my knowledge and belief, this is how our talk went on this occasion:

The Chief asked, "What is that pile of papers by your chair? Are you planning to start a bonfire?"

I said, "Yes, to your second question, as a matter of pure self-defense. These are communications from, or stimulated by, the Daughters of the Confederacy, recommending Stonewall Jackson for the Hall of Fame. They have been coming in for months, along with more modest persecutions in favor of various other candidates, and they are crowding me clean out of my study."

"What have you to do with all this?" he asked. "Give me a match."

I gave him one. "Some years ago, for reasons unknown to me, I was made one of the electors."

"Which means what?"

"Every four years I vote for seven of the candidates nominated, and every four years I get this kind of barrage."

"How are they nominated?"

"I don't really know. I think just by a number of people writing in."

"Do they work for their own nominations?"

"Oh no. We vote only on dead people."

He took a long puff at his cigarette. "Only on dead people. What good does it do them to be elected to anything?"

"Well, I guess it doesn't do them much, but it gives innocent pleasure to their descendants and others who admire their memories — like the Daughters of the Confederacy."

"I see," he said amiably. "It is always pleasant to make people happy, especially when it doesn't cost anything. Is this Hall of Fame a government thing?"

"No," I said, "it's private, but the letterhead says, 'Every American is a stockholder in the Hall of Fame.' "

"That sounds nice. As a stockholder, what do I get?"

"Well, if you go there, you can walk around and look at the statues or busts or whatever they have."

"At my village, after a really hard rain I can hunt around and look at the bones of my own ancestors. I never found that particularly interesting. When you're in the East, do you visit this Hall of Fame?"

"No."

He toyed with his handsome, Navaho silver necklace. "How do you decide whom to vote for?"

I hesitated. "You see, they're famous. You think over the list of candidates and the information about them that has been sent you, and you decide that certain ones are certainly famous, and the seven most famous are the ones that should go in."

He tugged thoughtfully at a lock of hair. "If they're already famous, why do they need to be put in this Hall? My great-nephew has told me about this Stonewall man, for instance, so even I know about him. But apart from the chance that among my more screwy acquaintances is yourself, and you've been telling me about it, if this man is elected would I hear of it? Would he become more famous, or what?"

"I don't think he'd become more famous, no. It's — it's a way of showing respect."

He clasped his hands behind his head and leaned back, smiling. "The more I learn of you white people, the more peculiar you are. You're always labelling things. You kill a cow, then you examine the meat, and if it's good, you put a stamp on it. A man dies, and if he's been good enough, you put a stamp on him, or sometimes you put him on a stamp and show your respect by cancelling him. A peculiar, peculiar people."

Some Unmined Gold

A VAST NUMBER of events and characters, heroes, villains, battles, bitterly-fought wars, astonishing negotiations, go ignored because they had little or no effect upon what we regard as the "mainstream of history" — by which we mean that part of it that somehow affects us. The "unimportant" matter may have destroyed a courageous nation, but that concerns us not.

For instance, to come close to home, had Armijo's final betrayal of Mexico not turned this territory over to the United States, but only to a powerful Mexican revolutionary, it, and the strange character of Armijo himself, would have gone completely ignored, at least as far as North American letters are concerned. As it is, the average North American historian assumes that his country would have taken over New Mexico eventually in any case. The non-battle of Apache pass, an incident of no slight importance, is hardly mentioned, Armijo overlooked.

Many similar matters and characters can be found in the long story of our subjugation of the Indian tribes. A few men, like Tecumseh, threw their weight into a war between white nations and threatened to tip the balance against us, or, like King Philip, did at least come within sight of the laudable aim of driving the Yankees into the sea, which would have slowed the flowering of New England, terminated Harvard College, and probably postponed the Supreme Court's decision on segregation. Therefore they get mention.

Our westward expansion was like a flood breaking through a long series of dykes. Time and again momentary twinges of honor on the white men's part or exceptionally effective Indian resistance held back the flood; in the end we always broke through. The Indian wars, therefore, appear as purely internal matters, comparable, perhaps, to riots in cities, but possibly less significant since they were never anything more than futile delaying actions against the inevitable.

For this reason general American historians virtually ignore the wars of resistance, the devious diplomacies, the amazing characters, and some remain untouched even by specialists. Armijo has had some treatment by historians of the Southwest as well as by historical novelists, the best of the latter being Ruth Alexander. The Indians and the white men with whom they struggled have often been left entirely to second-rate popularizers.

This column is written in the faint hope that it may catch the eye of some competent historian and lead him to handle either the history of Cochise and the resistance of the Chiricahua Apaches, or the history of the Utes leading to the Meeker Massacre, the battle of Milk Creek, and their aftermaths. Both subjects are of high interest, involve astonishing characters, both Indian and white, and badly need dispassionate research and factual (but not flat) presentation.

Both of these topics have been the prey of popular writers. I myself am guilty of a juvenile about Cochise, and this piece is sparked by a new book, *Massacre*, about the Ute affair. The trouble is that popular writers seldom handle these affairs as well, or as interestingly, as will a good historian.

Either story also reveals the extent to which the Indians outgeneraled and outfought our troops, and how we won in the end by sheer weight of numbers and equipment. The battle of Milk Creek is certainly one of the most humiliating and farcical defeats ever inflicted on regular U.S. soldiers by an inferior force. The Utes involved were not even sure they were going to fight until someone fired a shot, and had no one in command until after the battle started. All in all, it was an astonishing business, although no more astonishing than half a dozen other items in either the Ute or the Chiricahua story.

I recommend both to historians looking for a good story. They have been hacked at by amateurs, distorted by popularizers, but the real stories remain unspoiled and half-told. Either one is a natural for a man who knows how to get at, and present, the full facts.

Indians, Republicans, and John F. Kennedy

Once, in writing about New Mexico Democrats, I mentioned the political "mental abyss" certain ones exhibited. In fairness I must point out that we have now had waved in our faces a really startling example of low-mindedness among the Republicans, a deal so elaborate that even President Eisenhower became involved.

I refer, of course, to having the governors of thirteen New Mexico Pueblos or their representatives carry the sacred Lincoln canes to the Republican carnival at Chicago, there to put on Indian suits and receive medallions having the likeness of Abraham Lincoln on one side and Mr. Eisenhower on the other.

No one can blame the Indians who accepted, though we can applaud Taos Pueblo for protesting such partisan exploitation. The proposition was smooth, the use of Lincoln's name had strong appeal, participation in a major political event was most attractive, and the fact that the President himself seemed to be in the picture should have been (but was not) a guarantee that the whole thing was quite correct.

The pretext was that 1960 is the centennial of Lincoln's nomination. It is not, by several years, the centennial of his sending of the canes. The governors did not go to the White House, but to a party convention. They received the medallions from a staunch New Mexico Republican, the Commissioner of Indian Affairs. There was lots of publicity. The

whole business was the inspiration of the New Mexico GOP
campaign manager and was carried through by him.

Now, Abraham Lincoln really was the President of All the
People. In 1863 he was in the midst of the dire Civil War
that threatened the life of the nation. He was daily subjected to what should have been insupportable pressures. He
intended to win that war, and that the following peace should
be marked by malice towards none and charity towards all.

With all this, he had time to make some study of the Indian situation, and to resolve that, if he lived, he would re-
form the whole system. He had time to consider the vote-
less, infinitely remote Pueblo tribes, to confirm their land
grants, and to reaffirm their right of self-government by having the Lincoln canes made, which reached the several governors in 1864. This small act was the unquestionable proof
of a really great soul.

However we may like Mr. Eisenhower, we cannot seriously
compare him to Abraham Lincoln. Nor can we so compare
the Commissioner of Indian Affairs. Strictly in regard to Indian affairs, Mr. Eisenhower contrasts rather sharply with Lincoln, for he campaigned for the Indian vote, and thereafter
was completely unreachable on Indian matters. In this he
differed also from Presidents Hoover, Roosevelt, and Truman,
all of whom had fairly large matters on their minds, and all
of whom could and did give time to Indian problems.

Whether the Indians of New Mexico or of anywhere else
should vote Republican or Democratic is up to them. If I
were a Navaho, I'd vote Republican. You can bet your bottom dollar that the great majority of the Indians of the northern Plains, after their bitter experiences of the last eight years,
will go the other way, unless Mr. Nixon comes up with something exceptionally solid and well conceived. (An outstand-
ing Indian is running for Congress on the South Dakota Re-

publican ticket; he may well be the exception.) It is fair enough, also, for both parties to woo the Indian vote, here or anywhere else.

This particular incident is distressing for two reasons. The first is the use of dignified, sincere, serious, but politically inexperienced people to make party publicity. The second is the travesty upon the memory of Abraham Lincoln.

Actually, it begins to be inescapable that, as a matter of self-interest, New Mexicans, Indian, Spanish, and Anglo, should vote for Kennedy. Recently I received a letter from the Senator setting forth his policy on Indian affairs. It not only emphasizes his adherence to the fine Democratic Indian platform pledge but goes further.

Among other things, he says, "We will not rest after fine policy pronouncements by the Secretary of the Interior. . . . We would not tolerate a situation in which promises are made by the Secretary of the Interior, only to be ignored or even undermined by the Commissioner of Indian Affairs." This is a correct analysis and nice dig at the existing Republican situation.

Much more, his program for Indian progress and prosperity is not special or isolated, but part of his general program for progress and prosperity for the whole nation. He says, "Our Indian platform pledge, you will note, harmonizes fully with other, more general, platform pledges, such as that to assist depressed areas of chronic unemployment, to provide decent housing, and to inaugurate a Youth Conservation Corp. . . . The increased productivity of all these groups, including the Indian groups, which would result from our program of opportunity would repay the Federal investment manifold."

Note those words about "depressed areas." They touch us in New Mexico vitally. From Grazing District 7 just east of

the Navaho Reservation to the Colorado line and again near
our southern border are whole chains of depressed areas of
chronic unemployment, where, as the Burma report stated,
living on relief has become an accepted procedure.

In 1952 General Eisenhower proposed legislation to eliminate depressed areas. A Republican Congress killed all proposals. When a Democratic Congress produced a workable
depressed areas bill, President Eisenhower vetoed it, saying
that it would "squander the taxpayer's money" and "inhibit
private initiative." As a kind of back-fire, the Republicans
have urged, and Mr. Nixon now supports, a piddling bill that
could not possibly meet the need across the nation.

During the hearings on the bill that was vetoed, the present
Commissioner of Indian Affairs distinguished himself by his
opposition to having Indian country included in its coverage.
Well, he, too, is a Republican.

The depressed areas, usually defined as those where high
unemployment has existed for more than five years, need
funds to attract industry, to develop resources, and above all,
to train their residents in new skills and trades. The need is
fundamentally the same for the workless coal miners of West
Virginia or the untrained, semi-literate Indians of North Dakota.

It applies to the many parts of this state — more than a
quarter of it — where the taxpayer's money is now being
"squandered" (in the name of common humanity) on the
thousands of relief cases, where able men sit idle, and private
initiative is inhibited by a blank wall of impossibility to earn
a living under existing conditions.

The Democratic Indian plank promises "a program to assist Indian tribes in the full development of their human and
natural resources and to advance the health, education, and
economic well-being of Indian citizens while still preserving
their cultural heritage."

For "cultural heritage" read "love of one's home and one's traditions," apply the whole statement nationally, and you have the Democrats' depressed areas policy.

The essence of the Republican plank is that the new administration would keep on just like the present one, and the Republican-Nixon record on depressed areas, during the life of this administration and in the present campaign, is painfully clear.

Not without reason did Kennedy write to me, "It is hard to visualize a Nixon Administration concerned with the welfare of Indians but unconcerned about West Virginia coal miners, unemployed textile workers in Massachusetts, hardhit farmers in Minnesota" and, I do not hesitate to add, broken ranchers in New Mexico, who until recently made their own way and held their heads as high as any men.

Indian Agent, Old Style

THIS PAPER GOES light on Indian news, so the death of Chester E. Faris last Thursday drew a brief squib that many readers may have missed. Faris is a man who deserves much more than passing mention.

To me, he was the last of the old-style Indian Agents, and one of the best of them, although by the time he was appointed to the Jicarilla Apache Agency at Dulce, the term "agent" had been politened into "superintendent." He was a man who knew literally a thousand Indians by face and name, Apaches, Pueblos, Navahos, and who dealt with those under his jurisdiction as human beings, face to face and man to man. He was able to combine this human contact with first-rate ability as an administrator, paper-worker, and bureaucrat. In the early days of my own dealings with Indians, I looked on him as a teacher and am proud that he thought me teachable.

As noted, his first agency was at Dulce, where he was sent in 1922. At that time, there were about 550 Jicarillas left, almost exactly half what their population had been in 1890. Tuberculosis raged among them, abetted by hopelessness and dire poverty. Children were dying like flies, and statistically the tribe was due to be extinct, or as good as extinct, in a little over a decade.

Faris was sent there to wind up the estate, to prepare for disposal of a tract of Indian land that would soon be surplus.

He accepted the appointment on the condition that if he found anything that could be done to help the Apaches, he should have a free hand and support from Washington in doing it.

He found a group of men who were only waiting for a superintendent such as he — Wirt, the famous trader, Dr. Cornell, whom he and Wirt recruited to be reservation physician, and Sims, the Lutheran missionary. Alongside them were Apaches of character and ability, notably the late John Mills Baltazar. The possibilities were there.

With the help of these men and the essential resource of the innate strength and vigor of the surviving tribesmen, he brought about a revolution on the reservation. Like so many Indians, they had been prevented from helping themselves; he set them to doing just that. The group tore up the existing school and hospital system and substituted one such as had never been known in the Indian Service, perfectly geared to the Apaches' desperate situation.

They put the Indians into the sheep and cattle business, and closed out the non-Indian leases that tied up the winter range. Faris, long before the Indian Reorganization Act, encouraged tribal self-government and authority. The Jicarillas today are well-off with oil and gas leases, but that is recent. When oil was found, they were already moderately prosperous, enterprising people with a future that made life worth living and effort worth making. Tuberculosis was virtually wiped out in the early 1930's, and by the time of World War II the tribe's population was rapidly approaching its former high point.

It was all done without fuss or fanfare, and with real love for the people. Faris, by 1930, had moved on to the superintendency of the Northern Pueblos, and went later to higher posts, but he never lost sight of the Jicarillas. The work he and his group did stood solid, an example of the reality of economic development that I wish the present Commissioner of Indian Affairs would study and emulate. Small wonder the tribe named its scholarship fund, $1,000,000 of oil money set aside to send its young people through college, the Chester E. Faris Fund.

What other formal monument, apart from the fund, he may ever have we do not know. Informally, he has one of the most enduring imaginable — the survival of a people, the mere fact of whose children, generation after generation, must be credited to him.

Vidal Gutierrez

THIS PAPER HAS already run a notice of Vidal Gutierrez of
Santa Clara, who, according to the records, was born in
1859 and died at the end of 1961. I add my remarks, because
I knew this man for over thirty years, loved and admired him,
and there is much to tell of him that was not given to the
reporter.

If the birthdate given is correct, he was a young man of seventy when I first met him, wearing a stiff-brimmed Stetson with
a downy eagle plume in the hatband, his braids black and
long and neatly wrapped, a handsome, aquiline, alert man,
sitting easily in the saddle on a tall, white horse.

He had an excellent mind, was a notable storyteller, and
possessed a lovely sense of humor. He could, when the mood
was on him, keep the company laughing on and on. He had
a splendid singing voice, and had himself composed many
songs when he was younger. Only a few years ago I had the
pleasure of approaching his house and hearing his handsome
drum beating and his voice, still strong and young, pouring
forth a good song.

As the formal notice said, he did not hold office; that is, in
the civil government. He was, however, a leader, a shaker
and mover, whose influence upon his people was considerable.

He was a conservative progressive. He valued the old
things, the customs, the ceremonials, but he saw also that
change could not be avoided. In his attitude toward the two

things, holding to the good of the old and selectively accepting the new, he was not unlike such statesmen as Churchill,
quite unlike our present, self-styled "conservatives" in this
country.

A sound American will base both things, conservatism and
progressivism, on the Declaration of Independence and the
principles of the Founding Fathers. So Vidal Gutierrez based
his on the teachings he received from the old men when he
was young, the traditions and prophecies of his people. His
life spanned changes that were almost catastrophic, they were
so extreme, from a life close to the thousands-years-old Pueblo
pattern to the days of Los Alamos. This did not send him
into a reactionary tail spin; he was too adult for that. To the
contrary, he saw change as something to be accepted, met,
and guided.

It was forbidden for anyone to absent himself from the
pueblo without the governor's permission, a good rule in the
old days of warfare, but the warfare was ended. The rule
should end. He saw to it that it did.

At the annual cleaning of the village, the women carried
all the rubbish out in pack-baskets. This was absurd, when
they had draught animals and wagons to do the hauling. He
opposed the rule single-handed, and it was changed.

Thus it went, until, when he was nearing eighty, Santa Clara
adopted a written constitution, with popular election of officers by secret ballot. Then, he said, his work was done.
Thereafter, the pueblo should be managed by the young people, who could read and write and speak English. As for
himself, he would take it easy, and attend to his religion. He
was a devoted Catholic and a devout Indian.

He saw to it that those of his children who wanted it got
more education than the Indian Bureau would give them. He
encouraged them to modern ways of living, and to deep re-

spect for the traditions of their people. Illiterate, non-English speaking, he showed them how to take from both the old and the new.

About ten years ago, his children were worried because he would not stop farming. That year he planted wheat and beans, if I remember correctly. He rode to the Hopi country in the back of a truck, to help the Tewas there with a dance they were putting on. Latterly, he had to be inactive. Now he is gone. For me, he has left a big hole in life.

Lo, the Poor Indian

ONCE AGAIN the movies are advertising a picture in which the hero confronts "hordes," in this case "the hordes of Baghdad." In the curious idiom of that branch of show business, a "horde" is any number of men over a dozen, placed in opposition to the hero, whether alone or accompanied by his faithful little band. (In the latter case, no matter how unreasonable it may be, The Woman will always manage to tag along.)

As every schoolboy knows, horde comes from the Turki word "*orda*." It was originally used to refer to the Tartar tribes, which were whole nations, 50,000 to 100,000 people, moving about to pasture their flocks or for warfare. One of these tribes could muster anywhere from 5,000 fighting men up. Those, ladies and gentlemen, were hordes.

Eventually, under Tamburlaine, Genghis Khan, Attila and others, they swept over a large part of the sedentary world, killing, burning, pillaging and generally rearranging the course of history. It was at that time that the word moved into the European languages and hence finally into English, with the sense, not only specifically of these huge armies, but of vast, swarming bodies of any undesirable people.

The moom-pitchers promote a superdebased form of the English language in which their misuse of the word "horde" is only one part of a terrific collapse of meanings. Indian traders used to entertain themselves by telling tourists that such-and-such a tribe of Indians was so primitive that its members could not converse in the dark, as their language could not be understood without gestures. The boys in Hollywood have reduced a once noble tongue to where they can't ask "How are you feeling?" in broad daylight on the corner of Hollywood and Vine without backing up the ruined words with gestures and facial expressions.

They have equally distorted the facts of the world, and to a large degree destroyed them. They have invented a Catholic religion of their own, full of boxing nuns, crooning priests, and other interesting phenomena. History they have invented all over again, and they have even rewritten the Bible so as to allow Rita Hayworth to squirm her way through a Dance of the Seven Veils and emerge pure and saintly.

In none of this creation of a fabulous and nonexistent world have they been more solidly disgusting than in their special version of the American Indians and the history of our relations with them. Like the recent case of the "hordes of Baghdad," their Indians come in hordes. (It is a minor item, I imagine, that Baghdad was a great center of civilization until it was overthrown and destroyed by the Mongol hordes. That sort of thing would not cause even a moment's pause in Hollywood; after all, what's fact to them? They have their own world.)

We had recently "hordes of war-crazed Navahos." The Navahos were a fine, fighting tribe (and still are, in Uncle Sam's uniform), but if they had run around getting war-crazed, they wouldn't have lasted ten minutes. Well, that picture had them somehow besieging Ft. Stanton, over in northeastern New Mexico. Probably the script was originally written for Comanches, but the costume department was out of feathers.

We get "Apache hordes" at regular intervals. The Apaches

were the most unhordelike people that ever lived. Cochise, the greatest of their chiefs, who fought the whole United States to a standstill in twelve years of constant war (started by us), never had three hundred fighting men in his outfit. At the end, when the U.S. gladly accepted peace without victory, he had little over two hundred. Some horde!

When he and Mangas Coloradas formed their grand alliance to try to turn back the California column under Col. Carleton, between them they were able to dig up some five hundred men with which to confront over a thousand equipped with superior weapons and artillery. According to the movies, however, Carleton's heroic band was assaulted by hordes of savage Apaches, crazed with blood-lust. Oh yes, The Woman was there, too with her dress torn in the most attractive places.

What has never occurred to the MOOM-PITCHERS, and apparently not to the rest of us either, is that the Indians were assaulted, wiped out, broken, besieged, and massacred by hordes of savage white men. The white men were savage, in that nine times out of ten it was they, not the Indians, who wanted fighting. They were certainly hordes; where the Indians mustered a few hundreds, the white men sent in thousands. Against some forty Cheyenne warriors, went two brigades. Over a thousand soldiers tried to stop Nana with a dozen braves. We were the roving nomads, drifting over the face of the continent, out to conquer all and destroy any that made trouble. We, the white men, were the hordes.

It has always been a mystery to me why the movies, teevee, writers, and publishers alike should feel perfectly free to tell the most outrageous lies about American Indians. Not long ago, the city of Birmingham, Ala., made *The New York Times* print an elaborate retraction of one news story it had run, and slapped a suit for a large sum of money on the paper for another. Some day soon, I keep hoping, some up and coming Indian tribe will get wise and sue the socks off author, publisher, producer, director, actors, and what have you who flagrantly libel it.

These thoughts are brought up by a little lollipop that recently strayed into my hands, entitled *Only the Valiant* and written by a Charles Marquis Warren or whoever hides behind that name. It is published by Bantam Books, who will stick you for fifty cents if you should want to buy the thing. Don't.

It deals at some length with Apaches. The author early betrays gross ignorance by writing of the "Tonto clan" of the Apaches, and using the word "clan" as a synonym for "tribe." I mention that merely because it is symptomatic.

He brings about a concentration of thousands of Apaches against a small force of U.S. soldiers. The largest Apache concentration in history, I believe, was when Cochise and Mangas Coloradas joined forces against Carleton's regiment at Apache Pass, pitting some five hundred Indians against twice that number of white men. This was a characteristic situation, and, with their fine generalship, the Apaches would have won had not Carleton had artillery, until then totally unknown to his enemy.

Herr Warren's Apaches are tactical idiots. They charge, yelling bloody murder, on horseback, through a narrow pass where the soldiers' fire mows them down. When they finally get tired of being killed in this way they fall back and regroup. Their chief, in order to keep up their morale, arranges to have a couple of captives tortured. Then these Indians, the most unusual since Fenimore Cooper's, return to a frontal attack, only this time it is on foot. They are met by a Gatling gun, but that does not stop them, not until all but a handful are dead. This is Apache warfare! No wonder the white men won the West.

Among other interesting ethnological items is the clear and even elaborated statement that young Chiricahua Apache women were totally promiscuous before marriage, and that a young man who spent more than one night with the same girl was looked upon as queer. Another that will delight connoisseurs is that Chiricahuas never washed, but that when they got to smelling too unpleasantly even for themselves, rubbed themselves all over, or had themselves rubbed, with a grease that closed the smell in.

Local readers will be interested to know that Apache women wove blankets. Also that near the fort in this story there was a "teepee village of Cochiti Pueblo Indians" (honest to goodness) and that all the young Indian women in the village were prostitutes, but that their trade did not prosper, because, again, they were so odoriferous.

I am just picking out a few high points in this magnum opus. I shall forbear to analyze the vast ignorance concerning military procedures and customs of the United States Army that Señor Warren displays, but I must let my readers know that in approximately the year 1870, there was in the town of Oraibi a hotel, at which white men usually put up. That jewel I cherish almost as much as any in the collection.

Now, of course, teevee and cinema are not allowed to use details quite as gamy as those with which Monsieur Warren has seasoned his concoction. Nonetheless, this massive contribution to the American literary scene is only one little example of the calumny against the American Indians that is being poured daily, by all media, into the minds of the American people, to shape the reception that Mr. or Miss Indian get when they leave the reservation to go out into the world.

Horned Husband Kachina Chief,
Pillar of the Press

(EDITOR'S NOTE: La Farge having taken off for Gallup to look at Indians, we turn his column over this week to his friend, the Horned Husband Kachina Chief from Awatovi.)

TRANSLATOR'S NOTE: My great-great-uncle old-style uneducated Indian. He talk only Hopi, also Navaho, Tewa, some Zuni, Keres, and Supai. Understand little bit Comanche. I educated Indian, speak Hopi and English. Uncle sometimes hard to understand, then he get cross and talk in different languages, so gets more harder.

My old uncle say to me, "Come write down this pillar for La Farchi."

I say, "What you mean, pillar?"

He say, "Lots of words piled up on each other, like pillar to hold up roof."

I say, "You mean post. What you want post for La Farchi for? You fixing to hang him?"

"No. He old hand at hanging himself. Seems to like it. Pretty soon maybe Bead Spring City Planning Commission going to hang him."

"Then what this post for?" I ask. "You think he need to be prop up?"

"He sure do. All the time that man fall on his face. That man fall on his face when he standing up."

I say, "You pinyon," which is one Hopi way to say "You

nuts" only politer. He get cross and talk Navaho a while,
then he straighten out.

"Look," he say. "This man all the time sticking his neck
out. His neck to get longer and longer and longer, like that
spotted animal in your little boy's picture book."

"You mean giraffe?"

He say, "Oui," which is Hopi all the same like French,
means "Yeah."

He say, "That man get so neck-stuck-out, and so many peoples clobber that stuck-out-neck, it all bent. Get so that when
he nod his head he bump his chin on the ground. He in bad
shape."

"So you prop him up with this post?"

My great-great-uncle he say, "How that post get in here
anyway? I talking to you about words, we put them in the
newspaper on account this man play hookey. So I make his
words for him this week because I am old friend. What all
this about a post?"

Now I wishing I got bunch of languages to get cross in,
but all I can do is make deep Eskimo sigh. I incline to make
argument but no use because my old uncle a chief and must
always show respect. I say in English, "Okay; shoot, Luke, or
give pop the gun," and when he look at me funny I say,
"That mean, I am waiting for your wise words, oh my Uncle."

He take a lot of time rolling a cornhusk cigarette with that
strong tobacco he smoke, and light it and make four puffs.
Then he scratch himself a little and I see he thinking deep.
Pretty soon he smile.

"Guess we going to fool them," he say. "Now you write
this down."

(End of translator's note.)

The Chief's pillar says, "Greetings, my friends. Ain't going to be no pillar this week. All the Indians at Gallup playing Indian. I got to run now and catch bus to go there too. Good-bye."

IV
Farrago

Lilac and Holly Trees

THE STORM has come and gone, and it did a lot less damage than most of us feared. Santa Fe as of this writing could justifiably call itself "The Lilac City"; I would not, however, advise the Chamber of Commerce to push that title. It would be all too likely to lead to cracks about lavender that would do us no good. Or maybe puce, a word gone bad through aural association.

The loss of the white lilac tree in the Prince Patio remains a tragedy. That was a rare tree. My standard of comparison is a lilac in the township of North Kingston, Rhode Island, a limb of which was broken when a young lady landed in it on her way down from her window to elope with one of Lafayette's aides-de-camp.

At the time of her elopement the bush was already strong enough to break her fall and survive. By the time I knew it, it had reached a respectable age. Even so, it has not the massiveness, the quality of venerable vigor combined with femininity, that characterized the Prince tree, much younger though the latter was.

Lilacs back there have a lot of endurance. On a piece of family land are the ruins of a farm that, from what one can tell without excavating, dates from not later than 1820 and not earlier than 1700. The place was abandoned over fifty years ago. Of its garden, only the lilacs remain, run wild and spread to form a thicket covering about a quarter of an acre. Few of the bushes are more than shoulder high. They make their way in constant battle with coarse grasses, blackberries, and other stubborn plants, yet each year they spread a little more, and they bloom richly.

Hard by, the road runs for about a thousand yards through solid laurel, tall enough nearly to meet over the narrow road well above the top of a car. In alternate years the massing of blooms is overpowering. That is a harsh land with a thin soil, but it certainly breeds flowers.

Since lilacs flourish here, I wonder if we could not raise holly, which does very well in Rhode Island. That's a good tree. Its green leaves shine all winter and the snow on them makes fascinating patterns. In the spring the blossoms perfume the air all around, and they are great providers for bees. A bird that nests high in holly is relatively safe from cats.

To do well, hollies must have a satisfactory love life, and of course that is the kind of thing that creates difficulties in New England. Out here, hollies with a Latin touch, uninhibited hollies, so to speak, might thrive exceptionally.

Two distinguished maiden ladies in Rhode Island, distant cousins of mine, had a row of splendid holly trees, tall, noble of girth, wide-spreading, of which they were — and are — very proud. These trees never bloomed, but they were nonetheless famous, and with reason, by far the handsomest hollies in the state.

Some years ago a New York friend spent a week end at their place. On his return to the city, by way of thanks, he sent them a seedling. The ladies were rather insulted; it was, they thought, the kind of thing one might expect from a New Yorker. Still, one does not throw away healthy plants. They stuck the little thing in a corner where, while it was so pitiful and small, no one would notice it, yet it would count well when it grew up.

There's no way to tell it until blossom time, but it happened that the intruder from Manhattan was a male. Through it the two ladies, and possibly the trees themselves, discovered that the native hollies were female. The following spring that row of magnificent New England spinsters was solid with blossoms, and that fall they were thick with berries. They have been thriving with a new, productive contentment ever since, and the Manhattanite is now twelve feet tall.

Autumn Philosophy

HERE IS A phenomenon that occurs about this time of mid-August every year, and which takes me back into childhood in a melancholy, nostalgic way that is highly debilitating to the intellectual faculties. It dawned cloudy and more than cool Saturday morning, then cleared, still cool and with a light breeze running through the clear sunshine.

According to my private weather station on top of my window sill, to which Pogo has no access, at present writing, 9:45 ante meridian, the temperature is 68 degrees. All of which adds up to this morning having in it the first, pussy-cat-paw reach of autumn, the forewarning, the all but inaudible statement that summer will soon be over.

It used to come on Narragansett Bay, under a slight haze, with the water lying smooth and metallic awaiting the noon breeze and, in the distance, a reflection of light on the water like light on steel. Then you felt it, you heard the voice, and suddenly, for the first time since you came home, you realized that the summer vacation was not endless and no matter in which direction you pointed your boat's prow when the breeze came up, you were sailing towards school over the horizon.

For a small boy attending boarding school that is even more violent news than for a day scholar. All the other long endings of the year lead to vacations, even to Christmas, and hence are seen as beginnings or joyful interruptions. It is in this one, above all in the early August foretaste that drives a child's mind out of total preoccupation to look into the future and see how it hurries towards him, that he has his first intimation of mortality.

From that time on you never quite shake off the sense of urgency. There are only so many sails, so many rides, so much fishing left. Most public schools start earlier than do the boarding schools, which can dose their pupils more massively while they have them in their clutches. While we still had about a fortnight, the day school in our village opened.

It was an act of meanness motivated by the wish to make real to ourselves that we still had time, that it hadn't happened to us quite yet, to ride past the school at a gallop, yelling like fiends. You could see the kids lift their heads inside. They were our friends, neighbors, and playmates, but we hoped it hurt them, because in the end, we knew, we were going up for a long stretch while they would still catch crabs and bluefish, and later fish through the ice.

Now I am considerably past school age. I am not a winter-hater; winter has its beauties and its pleasures as much as any other season. Still, a day like Saturday awakens the old unease. It leaves me sad and restless.

Unquestionably there is more to this feeling than the mere after-effects of the very mild trauma of having to go back to school. This column has speculated before on the odd point at which we begin our years. Many peoples begin their years in the spring, the reasons of which are readily apparent. There is a good argument in favor of regarding autumn as the ending of the year and saying that the new year really begins when the crops are in, the ground has frozen, and the trees stand leaf-less.

My uncle, a remarkable man, recently published his auto-biography.* He divided his life according to the four seasons, and labelled the first part, not "Spring," but "Winter"

* The distinguished Jesuit priest, John La Farge.

— "Pars Hiemalis." He did so because winter is the time of lying fallow, when the land prepares itself for the periods of a man's active maturity — planting, growth, and the final harvest of his works.

This philosophy runs counter to the presently popular one, according to which a man should quit work at sixty-five and live on his savings plus a beggarly pittance from Uncle Sam. If he does not quit work, he is penalized; not only is the money he has been forced to pay in withheld but he continues to be levied upon.

The theory demands that old men end their lives, not with autumn, but by dragging through a sterile winter until death releases them from idleness. There is one thing to this — idle men die sooner. I'll take the autumn philosophy, and with it the sense of ending, of nostalgia, and restlessness that comes at this time of year.

Chowder in Rhode Island

FOR REASONS obscure to this writer, he has recently been encountering discussions of the proper way of making chowder. As a Rhode Islander and native of the chowder belt, who learned this important branch of the culinary art as it should be learned, aboard a vessel under sail on salt water, perhaps I can make some contribution to the subject.

As Alfonso Gould used to say, the first thing is to know what to leave out, and in this we begin with thumbs and tomatoes. Captain Gould was the best seaman, shipfitter, fisherman, cabinetmaker, truck gardener, and talker in all South County, if not in all of Rhode Island and the adjacent townships of those flatulently dull states, Connecticut and Massachusetts. He was also an expert practitioner of a number of lively arts, among them the refined humiliation of his enemies and the making of chowder.

Rhode Island looks down upon Connecticut and Massachusetts, and upon their conceptions of chowder. If you take what New Mexico thinks of Texas, rectify it to 180 proof U.S.P., double it, and let it draw 6 per cent compound interest in the Quonochontaug State Bank for three hundred years, you can form some faint idea of Rhode Island's opinion of the two Puritan states that all but surround it.

Tomatoes have no place in chowder. There is a thin soup, purchasable in cans, called "Manhattan chowder," in which love apples are an important ingredient. That is not chow-

der. It is a ruined, dissipated, tuberculous variant relating to chowder as a top-hatted and debauched scion of the Van Astorbilts seated in the front row of a leg-show relates to a Block Island sword-fisherman in the act of launching his harpoon.

Some cookbooks give a recipe for chowder with tomatoes, falsely labelled "Rhode Island." This is a vile, base, unwarranted libel upon the fishermen of one of the most sovereign states in the Union, disseminated by that Massachusetts fifth columnist, Fannie Farmer. The New England "longshore" and "offshore" men of the sea are descended from a long line of vitamin-proof ancestors reaching back to the early Vikings, and far be it from any of them to dilute their finest provender with something that doesn't even know whether it's a fruit, a vegetable, or a berry.

As Farney Gould used to remark, you leave out tomatoes so as not to ruin the chowder; and you leave out your thumb so as not to ruin your thumb. Once the initial phase of chopping the ingredients is over (and you'd best keep your thumb out of that, too), chowder is piping hot at all stages until consumed. It's unsafe for the human limbs and members.

The only man who could safely and profitably use his thumb in the improvement of chowder was Targee, a fisherman of Narragansett Bay. Targee was a taciturn man who played in a good deal of hard luck, and also was renowned for his pithy statements. It was he who, from observation one time when mending his nets, coined the expression "slow as a frawg in a taar barrel," since sissified into "slow as molasses in January."

He was also a model for all struggling husbands, as the following incident will show. Once when he was short of funds on account of a fishing trip on which, he said, he hadn't caught enargh fish to buy a paper collar for a laouse, he set

out again, undaunted, like Hemingway's hero. As he left, his wife stuck her head out the door of the early colonial mansion (1663), the peeling walls and sagging roof of which somewhat sheltered them and their school of youngsters, and said, "Targee! Targee! Ain't ye goin' to leave me some money to feed the children while you're garn?"

Without breaking his stride, this excellent man turned his head and silenced her complaints with the unanswerable, "What'd ye do with the quatter paound of cinnamon I bought ye week before larst?"

Educators and Educationists

I WENT TO A church school, and I mean church, chapel every morning, prayers every evening, morning and evening service on Sunday, so for me the issue of letting religion into public schools did not exist. As far as I am concerned, my later school years, six of them, were accordingly richer.

Now we have objections to the putting of Christmas decorations on public buildings. Church and State, it is said. This paper has taken up rather sharply the matter of totally eliminating religion from public education. There are, it seems to me, some pretty fine lines to be drawn, and before I draw mine, let me say that I have been a member of the American Civil Liberties Union for many years.

"Congress shall make no law respecting an establishment of religion, or prohibiting the free exercise thereof. . . ." There is one of the cornerstones of our freedom, developed into a wide, positive doctrine by our courts. But does this mean that public schools must pretend that religion does not exist?

At that church school, one reason why my grades were often poor was the amount of time I spent studying evolution, which was not taught, and ploughing my way through the Koran. There was no objection. Religious instructors who tell children that evolution is untrue or unproven — expressing either gross ignorance or mendacity — make me as angry as if public schools forced children to worship against

their beliefs, as the U. S. Indian schools did thirty years ago.

I would not see anyone forced to take part in any activity that violated his beliefs. This includes attending school on Christmas Day, on Good Friday, on the High Holy Days of the Jews. At the same time, I do not agree that separation of church and state should lead to sheer obscurantism.

Religions exist. Religions, including that dreadful one called Communism, are the most powerful group of non-material forces in the world. To pretend that they do not exist, or that Christmas is not coming, or that everyone should stay in and study during the Three Hours, is ridiculous. Some years ago in this column I objected to a state attorney general's finding that Christianity in general was implicit in this country. The attorney general of the U.S. took the trouble to say that my position "was extreme."

There is a further fact that anyone whose mother tongue is English is uneducated if he has not read the Bible. Believe or reject its teachings, the fact remains that the Bible is the greatest of all the international classics. (The Koran, a one-man job, does not compare.) Not to be acquainted with that great work is to be cut off from a great mass of international allusions and references. I do not see how one could teach English at the high-school level and not include a certain amount of Bible, just as I believe that an educated person should know the general theory of evolution (should we forbid this because, since some consider it anti-religious, it is an inverted form of religious teachings?) and have some idea of the major religions other than his own (if any).

Since, to the believer, God embraces all, there is mighty little knowledge to teach that does not affect one's concept of Him, hence bear upon religion. The extreme attitude of eliminating from public life any reference to religion, of any kind, is a form of know-nothingness. We need moderation in

all things, toleration of each other's beliefs and their expression, and an attitude positively hostile to mere stultification.

This writer has no better qualifications than anyone else to discuss the problem of public education, but in a democracy such as ours, public education is controlled ultimately by us all, so we should all think about it and debate it. I am one of millions who have been inclined to say that we had too much theory in education, and let's get down to teaching, but without some governing theory, some stated goal, education can be reduced to total sterility. It seems to me, in my ignorance, that certain theories have lamed general education in the United States, and that the cure lies in other theories — assuming, of course, in each case, that the theories lead directly to the practices.

Before all theory, it seems, comes the simple question of being willing to pay for what we want. We have been trying to get an educated nation on the cheap, in part by skimping on facilities, in part, and even worse, taking our thrift out on the teachers. Teachers are more important than anything else except students. I repeat what I said last week, that we should pay teachers, as well as members of our Armed Forces, more. Also, we should have more of them. Classes of thirty children and more should become a thing of the archaic past.

One hampering theory seems to be that the schools should perform what used to be the job of the parents — socialize children, teach them manners, teach them to make friends, inculcate morals, create interests. Of course, the schools have an important role in these matters, but when they take over the parents' work, they swamp themselves.

One result of this idea, combined with the idea that everyone must be offered the same thing, is that what we used to call "the graces," all sorts of pleasant extras that used to be inflicted on children in their free time, are taught as parts of

the serious curriculum. A great many bright children will, sensibly enough, use their brains to avoid work. This is a useful tendency and has resulted in many important inventions, but it can go too far. Unchecked, children will substitute sweets for food, get by, and ruin their physical growths. By the same token, a mental diet of easy, "graceful" studies will spoil their mental growth. The choices should be narrowed.

Then we have the theory that it is "un-American" or "undemocratic" to grade students according to achievement, reward merit, advance the able. Everyone must get exactly the same thing, the class must adjust itself to what is needed to carry along the weakest. The Declaration of Independence says that all men were created equal, and goes on to specify the inalienable rights that constitute that equality. We could never have won our independence had Jefferson or Washington acted on any such folly as assuming that all men have equal ability or are equally deserving of promotion.

In school and later, we have inequality through differences of actual ability and through lack of equal opportunity. The former is universal, inescapable, and has always been recognized in the American competitive system. The latter is contrary to the American scheme, and calls for remedying.

The child who comes disadvantaged to school, however, is not helped by a silly pretense that all are equal. He and the child who's had a head start both deserve the handling that will enable them best to realize their potentials. Above all, a system that carries along the loafer, the frequent absentee, the child that won't try, is vicious. Life is competitive, life is often cruel, and victory is to the strong. Schooling that denies this prepares its pupils carefully for shocks and failures later on.

We are confronted now, not with a need to make a Ph.D. of every American, but with a need to find all those who

should be Ph.D.'s, lead them to want to get there, and make it possible for them. The need is urgent. It requires that we abandon some pleasant dreams and, as the Communists are doing, base our education on realities of human nature. But to do as the Communists do is not enough — which is another story.

The educationists are really moving in on New Mexico now, with a massive attack on Santa Fe. The strength of their reactions betrays the fact that they are beginning to feel much more on the defensive, their nice monopoly much more threatened, than ever before.

To begin with, the term "educationist" must be defined. It does not mean an educator. It emphatically does not mean a teacher as most of us understand the word, and nothing that I say in this column refers to the teachers of our local schools, a sincere, hard-working, thoughtful aggregation so far as my experience with them goes.

Educationists are the bunch that dreamed up and now make important hay out of the idea that, instead of requiring that teachers be learned or thoroughly versed in a subject, they should study something the educationists call "education." They are doing their best to destroy that word, the meaning of which has been clear for centuries. They have gone far towards establishing the rule that in our public schools, a well-trained historian is not competent to teach history, a skilled and enthusiastic mathematician to teach mathematics, unless he has also taken courses in education. Not knowledge, not scholarship, but M.Ed. or preferably Ed.D. degree are the requisites for tenure and promotion.

Conversely, they also hold that if you have studied "education," you can teach anything, whether you have ever studied it or no, whether it fascinates you or bores you to tears. Happily, the fetish of the Ed. degree has gained almost no

hold in our colleges — hence we still have such attempts to undo the fell work of the educationists as remedial English courses and elementary math. If the boys have their way, however, they will drive scholars entirely out of the primary and secondary schools and replace them with interchangeable ignoramuses.

It is notable that no private school of any standing has bought their bill of goods. If a private school wants a history teacher, it gets a student of history with a desire to teach; physics, a scholar and enthusiast in physics. Hence, also, private schools are not afraid to offer courses in history, geography, English, and so on, instead of "social science" and "communication arts," meaningless terms devised to foster incompetence.

The educationists do not intend to lose their grip on the public schools, for if they did, the schools might start hiring teachers on the same basis as do private schools and colleges, people would stop working for those Ed. degrees, and the game would be up.

Now our Santa Fe school board took a very important step this fall, when it revised our teachers' contracts to put promotion on a basis of merit instead of pure seniority and to require study of subjects (not of education) as a qualification for advancement. This means that our board chose for competence and scholarship, a choice that leaves the educationists out in the cold.

It is a choice that many of our teachers must welcome as heartily as every parent should, although there may be a very few who have reason to fear it. Many teachers have said, all over the country, how much they would prefer learning more about the subjects they teach to having to return at intervals to the boring rigmaroles of education courses.

But the educationists are powerful, their hold on the education associations is strong, and the democratic processes do not interest them. They have sent in a team of lawyers to fight the school board and the people of Santa Fe to the last ditch. I hope the board will stand firm, and I feel reasonably sure that if they do, these invaders will take a whipping. If that happens, then our local school authorities in this small, old, sleepy city will have done a service to the entire nation — which is one reason the educationists are fighting so viciously.

These people with a vested interest in selling degrees of doctor and master of education and who have spread their organization through all our school system are getting steadily nastier as the public increases its criticism of their curious tenets. The latest and most glaring example of this nastiness is the outburst of a certain Dr. Bereday, now an inmate of Columbia Teachers' College — an educationist stronghold — against Admiral Hyman Rickover.

Admiral Rickover came to Albuquerque to do a fine and unusual thing, which was to insist publicly that a considerable portion of the credit that the country gives to him for developments in nuclear energy should go to our own Senator Anderson. His speech about the senator was totally generous.

He also made a speech in which he renewed his criticisms of American schooling, and in it drew an interesting and very sound distinction between "education" and "training." His statement of the threefold goal of real education could hardly be bettered — to pass on the knowledge of the past; to encourage those with creative ability to extend knowledge; and to develop youth to apply what is known to life's problems.

Dr. George Z. F. Bereday was in Albuquerque to address the New Mexico teachers' convention and undoubtedly he conceived it as an essential part of his assignment to help them stay contented with things as they are. Discontent — "Divine discontent" — is the last thing such people want. Why, the next thing you know, the public will be expecting its teachers to be learned and will be wanting to have its children taught subjects!

I do not think that he came with his attacks on the Admiral already prepared. Calling a famous man a jackass sounds more like the outburst of a little fellow who has lost his temper, but the learned doctor did just that.

Now we don't expect these educationists to understand simple English, not even when they are native-born. They communicate, or issue sounds, in a very special academic double-talk of their own devising, and have used that lingo so long that plain American English must sound strange to them. So it is no surprise that Doc Bereday entirely failed to answer what Admiral Rickover said, and instead, set up an imaginary speech and had himself a lot of fun tearing it to pieces.

Admiral Rickover has more than amply shown that he is a man of character and of superior intelligence. Such a man would never pretend that on the basis of a few days spent in Russia and Poland he was "qualified" (Dr. Bereday's term) to compare their educational systems to ours. What the learned doctor has forgotten is that there are books and periodicals in this world, and that a good many people are still well educated enough to read them. The Soviet and American systems have been compared in detail, and we have masses of solid information on what the Russians teach, how they teach it, and what their graduates know. Admiral Rickover had plenty of sources.

As a matter of fact, his remarks on Russian schooling were incidental. His important comments were directed purely at our present system. What he had to say about homemaking versus history, about graduating functional illiterates, and other glaring faults in our present system, is what increasing numbers of serious people think. The facts speak for themselves, the remedial English courses in our colleges are symptoms of a shameful disease in our schools. Comparisons with other systems are interesting and provocative, but if all he made were eliminated, nothing important would be gone from what he said.

Such considerations do not stop a man like Dr. Bereday. Those who disagree with him are jackasses. Into hands such as his we are to entrust the education of our children, the future, the very survival of our country. It is a startling prospect.

An educator is someone who educates people, that is, a teacher. There are many kinds of teachers, but all worthy of the name have two essentials in common. First, they enjoy teaching, imparting knowledge; second, they have some knowledge to impart.

An educationist is more difficult to define. Educationists study education as if it were a mystery, and occupy themselves with creating a vast, closed corporation to control our national school system. As a rule, they are apostles of mediocrity, and bitterly resentful of anyone, such as Admiral Rickover, who suggests that we should pull up our academic socks.

In order to make the difference between these two classes of people clear, I have been collecting various examples of the educationist in action, or at least giving tongue.

Long ago I heard of an educationist who said that there was no reason to teach children any foreign languages, since even without knowing any, it was possible to show the peoples of other nations that we loved them. I'm sorry I didn't keep the exact reference, the thing is so perfect of its kind, so completely displays the combination of ignorance and stupidity that characterizes the real, fourteen carat, prize specimen of educationist.

Just one such example explains why this breed kicks, screams, and calls names when its tenets are questioned, as in my case, when my former columns brought me such interesting material from teachers (and school board members) and a shouting, would-be menacing, phone call from an official of the NMEA. He was wasting his time. I'm not specially brave, but I don't scare worth a darn over the phone.

Another neat specimen I failed to tag was an authority who wrote a piece in *The Atlantic* a year or so ago, attacking the teaching of spelling by phonics (as, thank goodness, our schools do). That character actually stated, in black and white, for all the world to see, that it really made no difference if a child, seeing the word "jug," read "pitcher." The child had the right general idea! It is difficult to believe that anyone of even average intelligence could have said that in serious debate. In fact, I don't believe it.

To get a further line on the experts who desire to have complete control of our schools, here is an authority writing in the bulletin of the National Association of Secondary School Principals. He wants to do away with boards of education made up of laymen, such as we have now, because we, the laymen, "seldom qualify as experts." Instead, school boards should be chosen by the teachers from among themselves, with some PTA members in an advisory capacity only.

This Utopian proposal should be borne in mind the next time you hear educationists prate about democracy. (It is undemocratic to advance gifted children or give them accelerated courses. It is undemocratic to grade children competitively — that is, competition is undemocratic, which would certainly be a surprise to Thomas Jefferson.)

Incidentally, the thoroughly educated, highly magnified expert who wrote that happy proposal is a former director of physical education, and holds the intriguing degrees of Ps.D., Ms.D., and Hon.D.D. from the College of Divine Metaphysics.

One of the best touchstones available for measuring educationists is the quality of the institutions in which they are trained and through which they function. Here, what I have are only two isolated instances, and must be received as such, although various sources indicate that the same thing will be found true in many schools of education.

A series of articles in the Atlanta *Journal* on the University of Georgia's school of education developed that in a series of intelligence tests, education students ranked lower in verbal skills than any other group on campus, tied with pharmacy majors in mathematical aptitude, and ranked ten points below the average in general intelligence.

These articles raised a wild storm and the usual vituperation, but the educationists were unable to refute them.

In Kentucky, a legislative investigating committee on education issued a blistering report on the general state of education, placing blame on the Kentucky Education Association and the teachers' colleges. The president of KEA and chairman of Murray State College education department, as usual, objected to criticism by people who were not experts and tried to discredit the committee because some of its members were Catholics.

He had to admit, however, that those who prepared for teaching in his mill were required to take no mathematics or foreign languages. In compensation, he pointed out that it gave a course in bait-casting, for a one-quarter credit. This, he said, was "the kind of thing all our people need to be equipped to do."

English is our mother tongue and our principal means of communication for all purposes. It is the language of a vast and splendid literature. It is the nearest thing today to an international language. Educationists, dreamily enchanted by "language arts" and "communication arts," oppose any serious instruction in English. Here is one authority who believes that formal grammar cannot be taught before senior year in high school. We hear that idea repeated many times.

What it means, of course, is that you wait until speech habits have become well set and the students are well past the age at which all language learning comes easily, then you offer them a last minute, one-year exposure to the essential requirements for intelligible English.

Another authority says that "it is wholly immaterial and irrelevant whether the spelling, punctuation, and grammar are in accordance with accepted usage. . . . A contention by the purist in English that permissiveness with . . . personal writing develops sloppy habits is altogether unconvincing."

And here is another who is afraid that if children's errors are corrected, they will virtually refuse to write. All history is against her, but never mind. She quotes, with approval, an eighth-grade composition in which "only a few words are misspelled, only about 4 per cent, statistically speaking." She points out that, although the young writer spelled "stocking" wrong twice, "he had it correct once."

Obviously, the people who hold to these ideas, or non-ideas, either do not know or do not care what a language is all about. No matter what kind of "arts" you put it under, a language is for communication. If speaker and hearer, writer and reader, have not been accurately trained in the use of this medium, communication will become inaccurate, even dangerously so.

Of course, it is much easier if you don't correct your students. It is much easier to let it all slide. After all, most of them, according to many of our best educationists, are not really capable of learning much (that "democracy" again), and as for the others, well, when they get to college, let the colleges give them corrective English. For heaven's sake, you don't expect the schools to *teach* people things, do you?

I have been trying to set forth what educationists, as distinct from educators, are. I am not doing this just for fun, but with the idea that educationists present us with a clear and present danger, against which we must protect our schools. Controlling the schools of education, in which, as rules now stand, most teachers must take some training, they wield great power, increased by their entrenchment in the National Education Association.

I have noted earlier some dubious instances of the quality of schools of education. To those instances, I add the comment of the chancellor of the University of Chicago, that they are ". . . upon the whole a pretty shabby lot, very often divorced from the main body of the faculty and with dubious standards and frail content."

What image of a school do these people offer us, who say so often that education should be left to the experts, meaning themselves, and that none but members of their corporation should express an opinion?

Here is an elaborate study of 100,000 school children to find out how they spend their leisure time, e.g., at badminton, movies, concerts, or "soda-fountain camaraderie." As to its purpose, "If the study shows that skin-diving is more popular than had been believed, special pools equipped with skin-diving equipment would be useful."

How about a special room with equipment for soda-fountain camaraderie? There would be a life adjustment course that would really go over big.

In *The School Review*, a widely accepted expert on elementary education writes, "Some schools try to obtain greater achievement by tightening standards for promotion; other schools are asking all students to take more required courses in English, mathematics, or science. The latter forget that the best way to teach less science or less of anything, is to require all children to take more science, or whatever the subject is."

Will somebody please tell me what the learned doctor (of education) means? All I can see in his words is the old, familiar horror at the idea of teaching subjects. Back of that horror lies the realization that, if teachers are primarily required to teach subjects, there will be no need for them to go to schools of education, and the whole racket will collapse.

It is interesting to see how some of these people express themselves, to see what foundation there is for the famous historian, Morison's, remark, "No one who has not read some of the stuff printed in educational journals would believe the nonsense that these people write, or the horrible jargon in which they express themselves, or the shabby mediocrity of their minds."

Here is the dean, no less, of a college of education, protesting a critical book: "Without a question, both author and publisher have established theirselves in the minds who know what the facts are about the public schools in this country as an individual and publishing company not to be relied on."

No wonder they are hostile to the teaching of grammar!

Now we have educationists, and we have teachers. Teachers are not paid anything like the value of what they give, they usually are required to teach more students than they can handle, and on top of that to attend to all sorts of administrative chores. Every so often, they must go and make another sacrifice to a school of education, or lose their standing. And wherever they turn, the educationists are watching them, trying to extend their power.

Under the circumstances, glory be to the schools of Santa Fe, where spelling is taught phonetically, where there is at least a stab at foreign languages. At least our schools do not regard a bright child as a "mental deviate."

I do not by any means say that our schools are perfect — they are not. But they are in no danger of accepting the philosophy of a California educationist who said, "We ought to get a secondary school program to fit the youngsters instead of fitting the youngsters to an academic program. Are the schools only for those who read and write?"

Art and Science:
Hands Across the Seas

I T IS MY BELIEF that the strongest present influence towards international understanding and friendship, and hence towards peace, is the exchange and co-operation that goes on in the arts and sciences. This exchange has gone on for centuries, it operates of its own accord, and will continue to operate except when tyrants forcibly forbid it, as the Communists are now doing.

This comment arises from a letter on my desk, behind which is a considerable history. The letter is from the director of the Hamburg Ethnological Museum, which is the oldest ethnological institution in the world. It is a letter of thanks and friendship, plus the news of an extremely important manuscript on the pueblos of the seventeenth century which the writer accidentally discovered in Madrid.

Here is where this exchange started: Before I had even received my M.A., I secured the enthusiastic help of the then president of Wuerzburg University, Dr. Karl Sapper, in a project designed to disprove one of his theories. This experience opened my mind, or, more important, my heart, to the reality of world-wide scientific co-operation.

Dr. Sapper had a pupil, Franz Termer, a year or two older than I. He and I started the study of Northwestern Guatemala in the same year, neither knowing of the other's project. Since he was Sapper's man, what might have been a rivalry became a co-operation. When the Nazis came into power, Termer, by then director of the museum, was no longer free to travel. He stuck to non-controversial museum work, and on the quiet taught sound, anti-Nazi anthropology to a few trusted students.

Since he could no longer go into the field, he threw himself with enthusiasm into helping plan my last expedition to Guatemala. Shortly after that the Nazis clamped down a little tighter on him, and our correspondence died away.

Shortly after the war I sent him a copy of the book that had come out of that expedition. He responded by sending me a book I could not otherwise have obtained, and our correspondence came back to life. Up to this point I was heavily indebted to the Germans; now I had a chance to pay them back. During the war, of course, the museum could receive no American publications. Since then it lacked the means to subscribe to them. A very serious gap was developing in its working library.

It happens that I take some of these publications, and that my shelves were at that time overcrowded with the back file of them. I shipped everything that had come out since the summer of 1939 to Hamburg, and I now regularly send on my copies as I finish with them. This is a relief to my bookshelves and in no way a hardship, since the same periodicals are available in the State Museum.

So it came about that I, who am no great shakes as a scientist and certainly not in a position to make gifts to institutions, am painlessly helping support an important European center of anthropology. The whole story, and its present outcome, are by no means unique. Wherever free communication exists, the scientists are helping each other. People who have never met in person correspond intimately and do each other favors.

So, too, the popular books and the works of art circulate

from land to land. In all of this interchange there is no conscious propaganda, yet it is the most effective of all propaganda.

Intentional propaganda is always hampered by the fact that its intent is known and hence it is received with suspicion. The idea that large quantities of tourists make friends for a nation is pure myth; the reverse is and always has been the case, back to when the Romans toured Greece. The exchange among artists and scientists is an exchange between men devoted to matters completely outside of themselves, quite apart from self-interest. Probably that is why it works so effectively to bind together men of all free nations.

Myths on Early Man

Reading a pseudo-scientific manuscript the other day for a publisher brought to mind how myths, derived from some scientific theory, linger on. (As to the manuscript, the report in summary was "bilgewater"; the recommendation, "reject.") These myths have terrific vitality among the general public; they are likely to last a long time even within the science concerned, and they are booby traps for workers in related sciences.

The prime example brought up by the manuscript involves anthropology and psychology. There is some debate as to whether anthropology is a science. I'd rather not go into the question of the status of psychology.

The author of this manuscript had read a lot of the speculations of the Jung psychological-anthropological school. I say "speculations" because the Jungians seem to reach their conclusions via imagination plus pure reason working upon "common knowledge," without bothering to gather real facts; certainly without considering it necessary to have any first-hand contact with their subject.

They have produced, among many others, the interesting theory that early man lived in caves because he was seeking a return to the womb. They do not define "early man," nor distinguish between "early" and "primitive" man, but it's worth our while to do so. We can define early man as a creature having the faculties of speech and tool-making, living during the accepted Old Stone Age — the time of the Jungians' "cave men," a tag which appealed to the imagination — that is, up to not later than 20,000 years ago. It's a crude definition, but it will serve.

The myth that early man preferred to live in caves began among early anthropologists. Many, but by no means all, the first finds of early man in Europe were made in caves. There were several reasons for this. The remains of early Homo Sapiens, Homo Neanderthalensis, and others, are thinly scattered around Europe, Asia, and Africa, below the surface of the ground. There is no way of knowing where to dig for them.

The archaeologists generally go to work where chance, such as something being thrown up by a fox digging a hole or uncovered in a gravel quarry, indicates that remains are present. Caves attract explorers; anything might be found inside. Geologists, Boy Scouts, and witch-doctors have from time to time found things in caves that brought the archaeologists flocking. The extreme cold of the glacial period did drive men into caves. The first branch of Homo Sapiens in Europe developed a religion that called for painting pictures in caves not used for any other purpose. The archaeologist with an itching trowel and no clues, then, will take a shot at the nearest cave.

Out of this the myth grew. Early anthropologists were naive. They propagated it, and it spread widely.

Away from warm, arid country such as the Southwest, caves are unpleasant, damp places. Living in them leads to arthritis. Prolonged residence in one by primitive people would lead to an accumulation of smells that even they would find unpleasant. There would be a high incidence of disease. The fact is that early man, like later "primitive" man, preferred to live outside, in a shelter of his own construction.

That mode of life enabled him to change his camp often,

an important sanitary provision. He followed the game and
the running of the fish. True cave-dwelling, rare as it is, and
the related cliff-dwelling such as we find in the Southwest,
seems to have come later, and in sunny, dry climates.

The matter may be unimportant. Yet, out of the disproved
myth of the cave-hugging First Man, the Jungians developed
the theory of a womb-quest. From this they went on to an
elaboration purporting to explain a wide range of myths, and
finally constructed generalizations about the mind of early
man, and then of man, which are intended to be of fundamental importance. Theirs is the delightful occupation of the
ancient Greek philosophers, speculating brilliantly, with logic
and imagination, free of the mean and constricting bondage
of fact.

The People, Yes—and Politics

I AM REMINDED of the day I did not witness General Mac-
Arthur's parade in New York.

I was in an office up towards the top of Rockefeller Plaza
the day he came through in a blizzard of wastepaper. I was
with a committee which had a lot of hard work to do; no one
felt moved to break up the conference just to see the parade.
The remarkable beauty of the paper storm, however, so enchanted us that we did pretty well stop work for some ten
minutes.

It was sunny. The tall buildings of the Radio City complex
created cross winds, whirlwinds, air pockets, and up-draughts,
in which the bits of paper danced, circled, floated, rose, and
fell in sun and shadow. Paper was being thrown from windows far away from Fifth Avenue or from any sight of the big
show. The open areas between the great, plain-walled buildings were full of these multicolored motes. It was like a music-
hall director's dream of an enchanted snowstorm.

One of the committee members, the president of a university, remarked that he simply had to get in on this. He tore
up several sheets of a memo pad, opened a window, and threw
them out. Everyone was pleased and amused; yet there was
no one there with a good word for the deposed supreme com-
mander.

That little incident, without a doubt, typified a lot of the
turnout and the hooray. New York is proud of itself, it is

proud of the show it can put on, loves to be in the show, and,
like all working people, loves a good interruption of routine.
An awful lot of people turned out along Fifth Avenue simply
to see and have fun. They were throwing paper because everyone else was, for the beauty of it, and to prove once again that
New York really does a job of its now-famous torn-paper wel-
comes.

I suspect that a lot of people had yet another motive. It is
probably significant that a very large quantity of what went
floating around the sky was a variety of paper the proffering
of which would not usually be considered complimentary.

The motive in throwing this out may have been merely aesthetic. The stuff is very light, and translucent. The long
rolls, opening out, twisted in a really beautiful way, catching a
remarkable play of light, on the surface towards one or shin-
ing through from behind. The strips spiralled lazily, twisted
upon themselves, straightened out again. They rose even
above the high buildings, into the unbroken sunlight, to
gleam against the sky.

The motive, then, could have been merely aesthetic. Knowing New Yorkers and their humor, one wonders. It is almost
impossible to avoid the conclusion that a number of people in
those offices were indulging in a sly commentary which they
could be sure would not be wasted on their fellow-townsmen,
however much it might be over the head, literally and figura-
tively, of the man in the gold hat.

A huge turnout of crowds is a mighty deceptive thing.
Once it gets going, the turnout snowballs with people going
along for the ride. Get a big, happy crowd together, and it
will cheer. The ones who don't care will cheer along with the
ones who do. Steam it up another way, of course, and it can
turn ugly with equal insincerity. The crowd thing is easily
whipped up, but it doesn't mean too much. There was a good

deal of talk around New York that Mayor Impelliteri turned out the schools and encouraged the city to shoot the works because he knew that, the bigger the initial build-up, the quicker the general would be deflated and, as all old soldiers should be prepared to do, fade away.

That may or may not be true, but if I were General Mac-Arthur, or one of the politicians who are now so recklessly exploiting him, I certainly would write a heavy discount against the significance of the crowds, the shouting, and the waste-paper storms. I'd have my spies out making an estimate of what proportions of what kinds of paper were thrown.

In the election just behind us,* millions of non-Catholics showed their faith in their Catholic fellow citizens in general as well as in Kennedy in particular by voting him into office. With that behind us, it is time to take a careful look at what happened on the American soil of Puerto Rico, the latest development of which, covered by a brief item this week, was the announcement by one priest that anyone who had voted for Muñoz Marín must confess to that act.

During the campaign, the Catholics of the United States in various conferences, both laymen and clergy, adopted a broad and fine position in regard to the separation of church and state. I didn't see them quoted, but they can derive their authority from Our Savior's own words, "Render unto Caesar that which is Caesar's." Senator Kennedy's position was equally fine, in fact, inspiring. A number of Protestant churches would do well if they would take unto themselves and be governed by the same principles.

Just when it was likely to do Senator Kennedy the most harm, the bishops of Puerto Rico informed their people that they must not vote for Muñoz Marín, the leader of that commonwealth. American Catholics denounced this intervention.

* Of course, 1960.

Then the Vatican announced that it was the priests' duty to "advise" their congregations how to vote.

The bishops met the protest by a further announcement that to vote for Muñoz was a mortal sin and would render the voter liable to excommunication. I have seen no report of any repudiation by the Vatican of this coercion.

Time magazine, of course, played the story for all it was worth in its last issue before the election. How many votes the business may have cost the Senator, no one knows; certainly thousands, perhaps a much larger number.

Then we have this recent priestly intrusion right into the secrecy of the polling booth, which is something really frightening to have happen where our flag waves. It is a rear-guard action; the Puerto Ricans, overwhelmingly Catholic, are equally overwhelmingly American and re-elected Muñoz by 58 per cent while eliminating the newly-born Catholic Action Party.

Lopsided power of any one church is likely to tempt it into politics. The Mormon Church in Utah is quite openly in politics, in business, in the newspaper game, and there is pressure upon Mormons in the rural sticks to subscribe to *The Deseret News*. The Southern Baptists certainly made a powerful effort in the recent campaign, and, according to reliable reports, anti-Kennedy sermons were common in their churches.

No Protestant church that I know of, however, combines the two powers of confession and excommunication, nor does the Jewish. It is that unusual combination that makes so many non-Catholic Americans uneasy. It did not make them uneasy enough to prevent Senator Kennedy's election, largely because they are, on the whole, confident that American Catholics would never stand a misuse of that power; that the American Catholic hierarchy would never wish to misuse it.

The Puerto Rican voters gave their hierarchy a resounding,

American answer, and we may trust that they have pretty well settled the issue. We can hope that out of the election of Senator Kennedy, out of his administration, and even out of the unfortunate occurrences in Puerto Rico, we may come to an era of greater tolerance, mutual respect, and unity.

It is not possible to understand the true place of the radicals of the extreme right, who have been cropping up recently in this country, without a reasonably correct understanding of the proper meaning of the words "conservative" and "liberal." Those meanings have become blurred, partly because radicals of one side or another have tried to steal them.

A conservative is a person who wishes to conserve, that is to save existing values. As the British Conservative Party has shown in the course of the last 250-odd years, this does not mean that conservatives are incapable of change. There is a vast difference between a conservative and a reactionary, a man who wants to set the clock back.

Jokingly, we speak of people who believe that creeping socialism began with the establishment of a government postal system, or of inspectors of weights and measures; within the last year I did read some curious individual's statement that parcel post was socialistic. Such persons are Neanderthal reactionaries, in the common usage, and very different from conservatives.

An American conservative believes in the principles upon which his country or his state was founded. If he belongs in the Northern tradition, he will stand by both the Constitution and the opening clauses of the Declaration of Independence. If he is in the Southern tradition, he is likely to reject "all men are created equal," or put special limitations upon the statement (although it was written by a Southerner and adopted by Southerners as well as Northerners).

He will favor a rather strict interpretation of the Constitution, but, like the leaders of the secessionist states, will want it interpreted rather strictly. Northerner or Southerner, he will aim to conserve the grand principles of America.

There is nothing in conservatism as such that requires a man to be a Know-Nothing, to fear or hate persons of a different national origin from his own, or to stand for racial discrimination. He is likely, however, to draw a clear line between desegregation and informal, social intermingling. This is the point at which liberals often become confused, while the radicals deliberately treat the two, quite separate issues as one.

A liberal is much more favorable to change, goes considerably farther in support of race equality and related matters, has much less interest in preserving what has been created in the past and has worked well. He is quick to see inequities, even to seek them out, and when they are revealed, he wants them remedied. An American liberal, who founds his political beliefs on those same, basic principles, is within debating distance of an American conservative.

The image of liberals has been blurred by blurry characters such as Henry Wallace, who never did know where they stood. A genuine liberal hates Communism as violently as does a conservative, for the simple reason that Communism demonstrably stands for the opposite of everything a liberal believes in. The Communist drive in the 1930's to take over the word "liberal" was part of a well-conceived attempt to confuse and divide this country.

A conservative will look upon our involvement with foreign nations as a necessary evil, given the existing state of the world, and he will want to minimize it. A liberal will look upon it as a good thing; he will be much more hopeful that through international dealings we can bring about a better world.

When the two terms are used in their proper meanings, liberals and conservatives stand at opposite sides, but not at the extremes, of points of view that blend into one another. There are liberal conservatives and conservative liberals. Neither conservatives nor liberals accept the extreme prescriptions, right or left, which call for overthrowing democracy. A conservative may want to retain democracy for quite conservative reasons of retaining the traditional, the basic, the tried; the liberal because like an early and famous member of his group, he thinks that all men are his brothers, but in the pinch, both sides will react in democracy's defense.

It is worth-while to glance at the technique by which Robert Welch and his ilk capture attention, which is the technique of the Big Absurdity.

In *Mein Kampf*, Hitler frankly expounded the Big Lie. So far as I know, no one has ever labelled the Big Absurdity, although it is an old technique. The Big Absurdity, like the Big Lie, can be launched with the cold-blooded intention of deception, but it is as likely to have been born in a credulous and erratic mind, whose possessor is its first victim.

You find a youth reading Shakespeare and you state, with conviction, that of course Shakespeare never wrote those plays; the use of his name on them, the credit given him by his contemporaries, are all part of a conspiracy. Your listener does not believe you, so you look upon him with pity, and you cite some silly business about anagrams that prove that Lord Derby, or Bacon, or any one of a number of other people wrote the plays.

The youth is ill-equipped to defend himself and the proposition is so ridiculous that he cannot believe it would be made unless it had something in it. The truly absurd has a peculiar fascination. In our all too rational world, it is a relief at moments to believe the irrational. So the Big Absurdities appeal to many minds, in all of which you will find the same characteristics — either a degree of ignorance that makes them unable to defend themselves with facts, or a mental quirk that prefers to dismiss facts.

Mr. Robert Welch has launched a number of these absurdities. To say that General Eisenhower is a conscious and active Communist worker, that John Foster Dulles consistently served as an agent for Communism, or that Earl Warren should be impeached for conspiracy to destroy the United States Constitution is to say things so beyond reason that they become fascinating.

In users of the Big Absurdity, too, you will usually find the need for a scapegoat and an easy way out. We used to be a comfortable country, safely divided from the wars of an older world by two great oceans. Within a short time we have painfully been united with that older (and, we think, more evil) world. We confront long, grey, painful years of tension, effort, suspense.

Short, violent bursts of action we have known. We kept up the struggle of the Revolution for seven years, the Civil War for four. Different, and far more difficult, is it to emerge from another violent war only to find ourselves in a decade, and now another decade, calling for unrelenting effort and the ever-present sense of danger, and no relief in sight.

How much easier, then, to pretend that Soviet Russia and China are not really menaces, that we need not struggle with NATO, that we can happily go back to avoiding foreign entanglements and let all our allies go, that all we have to do is wipe out a domestic nest of traitors and all will be serene! Impeach Earl Warren, blacken the ex-President's name, jail a number of people I disapprove of, and we have it made! Then we can reduce our army, cut our budget, stop foreign spending, cut the income tax!

Glory hallelujah! Here is revelation that really amounts to something. It will end Communism, ensure tranquil nights, balance the budget, improve the digestion, eliminate dandruff, and prevent receding gums! A wonderful sense of relaxation supervenes, and another sucker goes Jack Acid.

There is the technique and the motivation, behind both of which lies the age-old phenomenon of self-deception. It is so much handier to hate someone within reach, someone at whom you might get a chance to toss a brickbat, than to worry about the men in Peking and Moscow. And oh, how convenient this all is for them.

Not being given to absurdity, I do not believe that Mr. Welch is a conscious Communist agent, although I could certainly make out a better case for that idea than he can for accusing Eisenhower. One thing is sure; if the Communists by now have not taken advantage of this golden opportunity for a fifth column operation, they should have their heads examined.

Meanwhile, all the big shot columnists have been springing up latterly, one by one, to announce their startling discovery that the American Negroes mean serious business and that the settlement of the race problem once and for all cannot longer be postponed. North and South, East and West, the guilt is upon us. We all share what the Greeks would have called the hubris of bringing a flood of Africans into our land and there keeping them in suppression and ignorance; now we must all make up our minds to expiate.

This is, to use Cleveland's phrase, a condition, not a theory. It's too late now to argue delicately about preferences. There are somewhere around eighteen million Negroes, they are here, and what are we going to do about it?

The situation does have its lighter side. Last Tuesday's paper had on its front page a picture of Governor Wallace pos-

ing as a phosphorescent jackass for posterity that really would
be hard to beat. He ran no risk, he intended to run no risk,
the University of Alabama is an institution of learning, not
a Confederate finishing school like Ole Miss., its students,
faculty, and trustees were against him, as were all the wise
heads of state, but there he posed, with a state trooper on
each side of him and his chin nobly uplifted, all ready to be
immortalized on a new Mount Rushmore. How is Alabama
for stone mountains?

Then, most beautifully, in the very same spot on Wednesday came the photo of the nice-looking young Negro woman,
Vivian Malone, walking in quiet dignity past a row of seated,
staring white men. This is what the shouting and the postur-
ing was all about. The contrast could not have been more
wonderful.

Behind Governor Wallace's noble facade is the reality of a
people fighting a final battle to maintain the prejudices and
the beliefs without which the core of their behavior, even of
their culture, for more than two hundred years past, is inde-
fensible. Let not smug Northerners or Westerners be too
quick to point the finger at them; we, too, share the guilt.
Getting right close to home, New Mexico may have no Jim
Crow laws, but New Mexico is a Jim Crow state, and there are
many parts of the state in which that Jim Crowing extends to
the original inhabitants and the first settlers of the state. If
you support Jim Crowing for one minority, in time it will
spread to others.

Behind Miss Malone stands the even greater reality of all
those millions of Negroes, a horrifying proportion of whom,
thanks to us, is all but illiterate, but all of whom have finally
decided upon Freedom Now.

None of this is fun or any satisfaction for us who have
grown up under the protection of a system of disguised apart-

heid. But it's here, and if we don't meet it frankly, it will catch up with us. The end in any case will be much the same, the big question is, how much hate and blood is to be required getting there?

The reality is making a total fool out of the intellectual jackals who long have prowled around the edges of race. They range from the most wild-eyed of the Jack Acid extremists, to whom anything but a guaranteed 100 per cent white Anglo-Saxon Protestant is anathema, to such creepy characters as a man named Carleton Putnam, who has exploited his impeccable descent from Old American Anglo-Saxon Northerners to give oomph to his pigmy campaign to "prove" by "scientific" evidence that Negroes are inherently inferior.

For peddling this useless line, he has been much honored, wined, and dined in such advanced states as Alabama and Louisiana. He is a slippery debater, who claims that he belittles no race but the Negro but, in his speeches, indulges a sly anti-Semitism that is insidiously effective. He prattles along, a "Yankee," so he says, with the stars and bars branded on his forehead by his own hand. What he says is most soothing, almost like a cool rag laid upon a burn, to the harassed people who listen to him — and there are none who suffer more harm from his specious preachments then they.

Meantime, white co-eds walked Miss Malone to her first class. Governor Wallace may have stood embattled against nothing (except flash bulbs) in defense of Southern Womanhood, but the young Southern women of today are worthy of their great-grandmothers whose tough heroism, beautifully disguised by femininity, made possible the long heroic resistance of their men in the Civil War. They know that they can defend themselves.

They, and the male undergraduates in a genuine institution of learning, having been given time to reflect, having been spared the deluge of hate stuff that was poured over the youngsters of Ole Miss., can recognize the future when they see it coming. Thus, as so often happens, left to themselves the young show the rest of us the way.

There are giants in this land of ours. We have kept them chained with chains they can break whenever they choose. We, the majority, are also giant — suffering at the moment from a touch of schizophrenia. A war of Titans we cannot win. Now is the time to make sense.

The Man with
the Calabash Pipe: VII

I N SELF-DEFENSE, a number of friends banded together to give
the Man with the Calabash Pipe several pounds of a very
fine smoking mixture for Christmas. As a result, not only has
his study become distinctly more fragrant, but he himself
seems to have mellowed. When I dropped in on him, he
greeted me with a smile, removed a gift copy of the *Somnium
Scipionis* from the chair across from his, and handed me the
humidor.

On top of this friendliness, he said "Happy New Year" in
a cordial tone.

I said "The same to you," and settled down.

A large yellow tablet and a pencil lay on the table at his
elbow. Seeing me glance towards it, he said, "I was trying to
write down just what I'd wish for that would give us all the
happy year we wish each other. I've been studying it for an
hour, and this is as far as I've got."

He showed me the tablet. On the top sheet was written
the single word, "Fear," the letters of which he had elaborated greatly with Gothic doodles.

"Well, of course, it should read, 'Fear, Freedom from.' Roosevelt had something when he included that among the Four
Freedoms, and when in his first inaugural he said that all we
had to fear was fear. A strange man, one whom it will take a
generation or more for history to evaluate, but a remarkable
one."

He tapped the pencil on the pad. "Our world is barred from even the relative happiness our parents took for granted by many things beyond our power at present to change. We can't, for instance, unthink the H-bomb, and Lord knows what machinations we'd have to go through before we could make really fresh, good butter available to all. Well, you can be happy when you are afraid."

He relit his pipe. "We have enemies who are to us a continuing danger. We also have friends, and we have our own strength with which to combat them. To recognize our dangers is one thing, to be afraid is another. When we fear, we bring our enemies into our midst; we do their work for them. A frightened man is a vulnerable man."

He paused, then repeated the last sentence. "I rather like that. A wise man once told me that one's fear is not the measure of one's danger. That is a very true statement and one which, if borne in mind, will often help to lessen fear."

He glanced at the slant of sunlight in the window. "New Year's Eve, and the sun is well under the yardarm. Have some sherry?"

I accepted, with some astonishment. Shortly he resumed his talk. "Fear is what had the French parliament acting like a bunch of children over German rearmament. That's a real paralysis of fear; they're scared of so many things that they are suicidal — like horses in a fire, when they run into the flames. You can't blame the French entirely. We haven't been invaded since 1815. In the last 150 years the French have been invaded and occupied by Germans four times, two of these in the last 40 years. Perhaps they think the Russians would be a pleasant change."

He paused to poke the fire. "As for us, we let fear drive us into making false accusations against the innocent, and accusing of being our enemies and on the side of our foreign enemies those who merely disagree with us. A ridiculous fear, instead of the steady appreciation of danger and preparation to meet it we like to think of as typically American, causes quite sane and decent people to join up with the lunatic fringe. When we do this, we are not merely letting the Russians make us unhappy, we are helping them out by making ourselves unhappy."

His pipe refused to respond to several matches, so he knocked out the ashes, hung it in the rack to cool, and set about filling another.

"This country," he said, "has always dealt in buoyant self-confidence, to a point that often distressed weary inhabitants of the Old World. After Pearl Harbor, when everything looked perfectly awful, our mood was determination backed by sound anger. There were some who ran around screaming, like the poor refugees from California who streamed into Santa Fe, but nobody paid them mind. It's not like us to become enslaved by fear, make ourselves miserable, and use fear as an excuse for committing indecencies against our fellow citizens."

A surprised look came over his face. "Lordy! That sounds like a stump speech. Anyway, what it all boils down to is that I shall drink 'courage' to us all, for that is the road to a happy year."

Wilderness:
The Public Be Damned

As usual, after the New Mexico state legislature has come and gone the editorial post-mortems ensue, along with the summaries of legislators, political leaders, and columnists, and all you need to do is to read some of these, let alone looking over the legislature's actual performance, to realize what a mixed and curious record has been made.

It seems to me that one of the last legislature's zaniest acts was passing that memorial against the bill pending in Congress, to continue our system of wilderness areas. The quaintness of this act is underscored by the total failure of the legislature to act, or the governor to recommend action, on the bill for the development of chronically depressed areas — a bill that can, if it should become law, enormously facilitate such important proposals as those for bringing the northeastern corner of New Mexico back to life.

The impression I get is that if you come up with a proposal that might just possibly hinder someone powerful from making yet more money, our legislators will smack it down, while if you come up with something that will be a pure benefit to the whole state, they are unable to reach out a hand toward it. That impression is exaggerated; our legislature is not that poor, although why our new governor let that depressed area measure slide right by him (his attention was amply called to it) is beyond me.

As to the wilderness bill, the legislature as a whole was bemused, I imagine, by the great concert of misrepresentations behind it. Wilderness areas, if all those proposed were so classified, would set aside out of the national parks and forests that are already the property of all the people, not of any state nor of any one interest, a tiny percentage to be kept really wild, so that we ourselves, and our children, may continue to know the pleasure of real camping and travel in wild country, so that Americans of the future may, when they wish, see what the primeval country was like when their forebears first met it.

A number of Indian tribes were lured into opposing the bill through the plainly dishonest exploitation of a stupid mistake made by the proponents of the original form of a wilderness bill, introduced in the last session of Congress. That first bill would have made it possible to set aside wilderness areas in Indian reservations without the Indians' consent. It met quick opposition from Indians and pro-Indian associations alike and was quickly amended. There is nothing like that in the present bill.

There are always certain elements that cannot accept the idea that public property is for all the people, not just for them to exploit. In Arizona, there are certain large-scale, lowland farmers who, having exhausted the underground water, have now lifted their eyes unto the hills, which are in the national forests. They have reached the remarkable conclusion that the tree-clad mountains retain water, that if the trees were all cut down and the mountains, preferably, covered with a smooth, plastic substance (this is no joke), all the mountain rainfall would run down onto their farms, thus solving their problem. And what is that water for, why do those mountains exist, if not solely for the benefit of the farmers? That which I make money out of is real and practical; that which does not directly enrich someone is of no account.

Some of our New Mexico cattlemen resemble those Arizona farmers. If they could have unrestricted use of the national parks and forests — your and my property — they could run a lot more cattle. Some of the forest areas are set aside for sustained-yield timber cutting, beneficial to the woodland growths, and everywhere grazing is held down to ensure adequate reproduction of trees. In some places, mining is going on. These uses may be practical, but the cattlemen look upon them dimly.

What is much worse is that the national parks are set aside entirely for the recreation of the people as a whole, and recreation is one of the chief uses of the forests. For this they have no use at all. As to legislation that would take even an acre of land entirely out of commercial exploitation, on principle that must be fought to the last ditch.

The public be damned is an old, famous, and tested motto. Here it comes again. There is a never-ending, many-faceted campaign, often conflicting with itself, going on to get possession of the people's forests. It is alert and vigorous. It cares nothing for the widespread, very solid benefits to the whole community of these great protected, public areas. That is why there was such a great pother of propaganda against a wilderness bill as our legislature was assembling, ending in misguiding the legislature into voting against the state.

Here is a report by something called "The New Mexico Land Resources Association," which appears to be a very high-powered organization for grabbing off national land resources, a document now being circulated privately, later to be loosed upon an unsuspecting public. The Association has a high-class membership, a frighteningly powerful membership; its existence is a challenge to the common voters.

In a suave, deceptive way this report repeats all the old outcries about the amount of land in New Mexico owned by the federal government, and indeed, how that wicked govern-

ment owns land all over the country. As usual, the figure is
handsomely padded by counting in 6.3 million acres of Indian land — oh those greedy Indians! — and there is a moving passage about the wickedness of setting further lands aside
for Indians. Indians are supposed to die off, and it's mean
of them to refuse to do so, and to want to eat. Nowhere, of
course, will you find any indication that what the nation owns
belongs to the people of the nation.

There is that rotten old Taylor Grazing Act and other laws
and regulations under which the uses of all public lands are
carefully controlled, the number of cattle grazed per acre is
restricted, local residents have special rights, mining has to
be according to certain rules. All this is unnecessary, it says
here, burdensome, and expensive. Worst of all, neither the
state nor private operators make nearly as much money out of
these lands as they should. Next time you fish in a national
forest, or picnic, or hunt on public land, let your heart bleed
for those deprived investors. Slyly, the report even hints that
national ownership of these lands is socialistic. Dear, dear.

The Association wants to "crystalize the thinking — of the
citizens of New Mexico towards the formation of a definite
policy." Gentlemen, most of us are crystalized towards a definite policy — those lands are ours, we intend to keep them.

This report gets down to brass tacks when it says that neither state nor federal ownership "affords security of tenure
or use to the livestock industry . . . on a comparable basis to
fee ownership."

Then the tacks get even brassier. All public domain land
on which there is grazing should be turned over to the state.
Remember, state lands are now closed to recreational uses;
federal lands are not. Federal lands may be opened to a variety of uses, including homesteading. You bet their use under
permits is not comparable to fee ownership.

But we don't stop there. All of the national forests not ac-

tually covered by tall trees or containing watersheds essential
to interstate streams should also be turned over to the state.
And it says here that this means that the state would get
sixty-five per cent of the present national forests. Oh boy,
what a grab!

The project does not stop there. We are dealing with big
business, including our old friend the fast-billing Public Service Company (is there sarcasm in that title?), two railroads,
good old five per cent Southern Union Gas, big mining interests, the cattle growers and wool growers, and the State Land
office, that dedicated servant of all the people. These characters think big.

The people's lands are to be handed over to the state,
which, as we know, never yields to mere political pressure in
such matters. The state is then to pass laws under which the
lands may be bought (oh beautiful fee ownership!) for modest prices, payable in installments over fifty years at a very
low rate of interest. Oh baby! America is a capitalistic
country, and he who has capital should get the marbles. To
him who hath shall be given.

All of this document is laced with a wonderful tenderness
for the revenues of the state of New Mexico. If the members
of the Land Resources Association are so concerned about
state funds, wouldn't it be natural for them to start agitating
for a higher income tax? But of course, they would have to
pay part of that, and that's not thinking big.

From Halley's Comet
to Echo I

LIKE MANY OTHER families, I am sure, we have been sitting
out in the evening to see Echo I pass across the sky. Perhaps other satellites have been visible, but this is the first
that I have watched, and as I watched it, I could not help
but think how much has happened in the short span of my
life, a little less than sixty years.

Less than a year after I was born, the Wright brothers
made the first flight at Kitty Hawk. When I was a boy, auto-
mobiles were still in competition with horses, chugging over
dirt roads. The people in them wore goggles and dusters. The
cars frightened our horses and were forever killing dogs and
chickens.

Now we have vastly improved our roads and our cars. The
horses survive, for special uses, but you seldom see them on
the main roads and those you do see take cars as calmly as
they take chamiso bushes. You can travel now in smooth,
dust-free comfort, and in smooth, dust-free comfort you can
be killed. Chickens keep out of the way, and it is a rare day in
which the newspaper does not report at least a couple of people dead on the highways. This is a great step forward, like
pulling down the Nusbaum house.

Even when I was a young man, the sight of an airplane
was a rarity. In World War I, they were the symbols of a
fabulous gallantry, their role as yet uncertain. The Kaiser
sent his Zeppelins from time to time to drop a dozen smallish

bombs on London, and we wondered at the horrors of modern war.

I lived part of the time near Newport, R. I., and after that war occasionally saw the Shenandoah or a Navy blimp in the distance. I also saw square-rigged vessels and four- and five-masted schooners that were functional, profitable means of hauling cargoes.

The first time a plane came over our house, my mother was making wild grape jelly. She and the cook ran out to see the plane, forgetting their task. When they got back to the kitchen, they found that they had made a rather interesting and novel form of jam.

I travelled horseback in the forests of the May country in Mexico and Central America, seeking ruins. Now you fly in. It used to take at least two very tough weeks to get from the coast to the great ruin at Tikal; recently an acquaintance of mine at Harvard flew down there for the week-end.

In World War II, I landed in the Army Air Forces, and had the good luck to be able to be at least an onlooker with a particularly good seat at the great age of military aviation. I rode in the DC-4's which were the last word in air transportation (I am sick of the cliché to which the newspapers still cling, "flying boxcars"), and in one B-29, which was absolutely the last word in long-range, "very heavy" bombers — and the last of the small bombers.

Near the end of the war, I saw a jet do its tricks. That model, which went by so fast it took your breath, is long obsolete, and for many military uses, aircraft of all kinds are on the way to obsolescence.

The Titanic had a wireless, with which it could call over a short radius to other ships. Shortly there were crystal sets and headpieces. Now TV brings the movies (I remember Mary Pickford) into the living room, and, thrown up to fantastic distances in machines beyond the wildest imaginings of Jules Verne, pictures the whole world for us and spies out the secrets of space. Selected men are now in training for space flight, and selected women are standing by for the same purpose.

It is hard to take it in. My morning coffee still tastes the same, a quiet trout stream still has the same charm, what is unchanged and what is radically new are so mixed together that the very nature of our lives becomes hard to analyze. And, yet, hour by hour and day by day, most of us live in a battered, reduced version of the ways of our grandparents. But the satellites move overhead, one takes the children out to see Echo I, as once I sat up to look at Halley's Comet, and going back to the familiar room and the electric light that we now all take for granted, I wonder what the shape of my child's daily life will be, what hopes and terrors and marvels will give it its tone.

Fast Communications

THERE IS A SAYING that goes back to the Greek, that evil communications corrupt good manners. What fast communications may do to manners I know not, except that they don't improve them, but they are certainly hard on the nerves.

By fast communications I mean those devices, beginning with Alexander Graham Bell's fiendish invention, by which one can be reached in one's home at any hour, instantly. I mean those devices by which, if one is fool enough to expose one's self to all that comes over the idiot box and other media, one can have the news bounced off one's head all day long in short takes like being pelted with so much gravel.

What gets me off on this is the constant advertising the telephone system is putting out these days urging the delights of having a telephone in every room, so that no matter where you are you can be reached without delay. This advertising is fortified by four-color illustrations of smiling people who are simply delighted to be called while mixing a dish in the kitchen, working at the Sunday relaxation workbench, in bed, or where have you.

I have yet to see an ad portraying the pleasure experienced by anyone (even Dagwood) at being telephoned in the bathtub, but I know there are spastic souls who arrange for this. They are not to be confused with those relaxed characters who use a nice, warm bath as a center of operations, a tradition that goes back to ancient Rome.

Now my experience is that to be telephoned in the middle of the night is extremely disagreeable, and in the course of a now moderately long life, I cannot remember a night call that was of any importance at all. It is also my observation that the happy housewife, when she hears the phone ring just as she is scrambling an egg, will yell to little Johnny or whoever happens to be near to take the call, and *don't* say I'm in, and ask who it is.

Which leads me to remark incidentally that there has, so far as I know, never been an instrument that could compare to the telephone for making liars out of adults and little children.

Of course, your nearest and dearest may be snatched from this vale of tears at midnight, but, to be brutally honest about it, the remains will keep until the news can be brought to you as it used to be brought to our ancestors, and, as far as you are concerned, there will be no difference.

I have lived for extended periods of time where the mail came only once a week, where there was no telephone within several days' travel, and where the telegraph was a tenuous and very expensive means of sending really important communications fast. I had little use for the telegraph. As for the news, the news of home in letters, the news of the world, coming in weekly and usually from ten days to a fortnight old, it was just as fresh, just as timely, as if our "modern (ugh!) magic" had pelted me with it at the moment it happened.

When my partner and I saddled our horses and took a trip, we were unreachable. If we were away on a mail day, we just let the mail await us. We spent almost all our time on worthwhile activities, and once a week for several hours we suffered the intrusion of the outside world, enjoyed tidings of our families and friends, and that evening talked things over.

That was the way people lived a century ago, and from then

back to the beginning of time. If some goon wanted to rout you out in the middle of the night, he made a row outside your door and you sent for the watch or dumped a pail of something on his head. Now, if you are suckered in by those winning pictures, all he has to do is dial your number, breathe hard down the phone, hang up, and repeat at intervals.

The phone company, as a matter of fact, has in recent years introduced one improvement that ranks even higher than its new, intelligible mode of billing. It has telephones on which you can silence the bell. This means that if you wish, you can have that thing by your bedside and it will be your servant, available when you want it, but powerless to strike when you wish peace.

The Man with
the Calabash Pipe: VIII

"CHEESE," said The Man with the Calabash Pipe, "Cheese!" and waved his cup so that it nearly spilled.

He had come for the purpose of taking tea with me, and he is as finicky about his tea as he is haphazard in regard to the fuel he stuffs into his pipes, and why he should suddenly talk about cheese I could not figure.

"No," he said, reading my mind. "I'm not going off my head. I was remembering a column you did a week or so ago on the flavorless foods we eat nowadays, and I was wondering why you had so little to say about cheese. Have you ever had any experience in trying to get a good, runny Camembert in an average American restaurant?"

"Yes," I said, "I didn't have much luck."

"Pasteurized cheese spreads," he said, making a sour face. "Blends, smoked odds and ends with pimiento . . . It's distressing, and yet, this country is the originator of one of the world's heartiest cheeses, Liederkranz, a real, upstanding, outgiving, cheese-lover's cheese." He sniffed at the tea, said, "Good, no jasmine," which I considered an insult, and took a hearty swig. "The man with the grey flannel suit may pass, but I fear that the man with the grey flannel palate is here to stay."

Glancing out of the window his attention was caught by the unusual sight, possible only in the kind of weather we've had this week, of a robin with snow falling around him, pulling a worm out of the ground.

"That worm," he said, "how much better for it if it had been slothful! 'The early worm gets the bird,' you know." He emptied his cup and handed it over silently for more.

"There's another sorry change," he said, "no doubt one of the causes of our juvenile crime waves — no longer are the sterling maxims of our ancestors seared into children's brains as they toil over copy books. How many times, as a punishment for being late, have I sat and written 'Too many swallows make a fall' over and over."

He had a swallow of tea. "Nice stuff," he commented, "not much spring in it, but doesn't make falls either. Our characters were shaped, our lives guided, by those maxims imprinted in our young brains. 'Honesty is its own reward' — fair warning to one and all, cynical but true. 'A penny saved is pleasure spurned.' "

I said, "I must admit that I am much guided by 'Never do today what you can put off till tomorrow.' "

"Precisely," he set down his cup and pulled out his pipe, "but of course, some of them need to be brought up to date, such as, 'It's a straight lane that leads to Miltown.' But one who follows your principle will never travel it."

"How about the Spanish?" I asked.

He beamed. "Wonderful proverbs — 'Panza llena, medicos contentos.' That's hard to beat. And don't forget the Latin; many a critic has made his fortune on 'De gustibus nil nisi bonum.' "

He paused to light his pipe and surround himself with a cloud of smoke vaguely suggestive of a burning bush in a spring snowstorm.

"We have so many valuable proverbs about time," he said. "There is a pair that everyone should take as a guide. The first one is, 'Punctuality is the thief of time.' Never forget it. It's companion is, 'Procrastination is the vice of princes.' "

"Yes," I said, rising to collect the tea things, "and 'Prevarication is the virtue of diplomats.' Are you ready for sherry?"

He murmured, "One swallow will not make a fall."

Love and a Season

THIS COLUMN appears on the old Yule, the shortest day of the year, the solstice — which means, the day when the sun stands. Now it ends its retreat to the south, and though the fiercest days of winter are yet to come, from now on darkness will be in retreat. All over the world men take special note of this day, Christians less than others, because four days later we celebrate the coming of an even greater Son.

The ancient, almost universal rituals over the sun's turning back are a curious evidence of what makes man's mind human. Animals, even plants, responsive as they are to the amount of light they receive, undoubtedly are affected in some way by the reversal of the sun's progress. To the ordinary observer, however, they are apparently affected only by the return of warmth, months later. Certainly they show no awareness of the slowly lengthening days.

So, for millions of years, it must have been with man's progenitors. Not until ancestral man was able to make conscious note and to remember what he had observed, even when it did not immediately affect him, would he pay attention to the fact that the sunrise ceased to move south and began coming back north again. Without clocks or any even moderately precise measurement of time, mind, reason, memory, had to go far beyond the brute before men could recognize that this change in position was the cause of a change in the length of the day which was not apparent until some little time had elapsed.

To develop this into the kind of occasion humans recognize, with ritual and social implications, was, of course,
quite beyond the aboriginal animal. Speech and transmitted,
as against individually retained, memory were requisite. That
ritual should be included meant that already man was attain-
ing the highest of his attributes, that faculty of projecting his
imagination beyond experience, beyond the knowable, which
makes religion possible.

The animals take life as it comes. Man can think into the
future; in a limited sense, he can forecast a lot of future
events. As a result, he is an utter worry-wart, at least in comparison to the beasts. Having recognized the significance of
the sun's return, having rejoiced in it, having celebrated it, it
was typical of him that he should begin one day to worry
lest the sun might decide not to return some year. That
lively imagination of his offered some hair-raising suggestions
as to what would happen if it did not.

That particular fear is possible only at a relatively low level
of religious evolution, when the sun is conceived of as an independent, arbitrary god in itself, or the creature and servant of
a god or gods capable of the most cruel whimseys. It had the
effect of pointing up the solstice more than ever, in any case,
and undoubtedly had strong after-effects on the manner and
intensity of the celebrations of later, more advanced peoples.

To us, now, the solstice is no more than a natural phenomenon. We know that it will recur, just as we know that these
major and minor natural recurrences of which the process of
the universe is composed, the "natural laws," are among the
most spectacular of all evidences of the Creator's greatness.
It is still a date to be reached with satisfaction. As far south
as we are, the days are never really short, but they shrink
more than enough. That four days before the most joyful of
all our feasts they should start to lengthen is an addition, a
bonus, for the season of joy and generosity.

I should not care to have my home in the southern hemisphere, where it is Midsummer's Day that occurs on December 21, and thereafter the sun is in retreat. I have lived in the summer lands where snow is unknown and occasional cold spells are taken as personal insults, and have passed Christmas Eve sitting at ease with friends on a balcony, breathing the soft air and watching the rockets. Anybody who wants it can have it.

This column comes out on the old, heathen Yule of the Norsemen. We shall burn their log later, on Christmas Eve, to ensure that Santa Claus has a cozy chimney to come down a little later. May everyone who reads this be warm over those days, happy over an amplitude of giving, replete with receiving, mellow with good eating and drinking, rich with love.

It was my plan, for the Sunday between Christmas and New Year's Day, to produce a column suitable to the season. I had a lot of nice words lined up in my head, and was all set to go, but instead, a son was born to us over the period of the paper's deadline, and that was that.

The coincidence of the child with the holiday period, and the New Year right afterwards, leads one to think more deeply than usual upon the new year and upon our time. This is a strange world into which to bring new human beings, a world so full of misery, and so full of dreadful danger to us who still, by God's grace, live in happiness, freedom, and comfort.

We are all of us in some measure responsible for the state of the world. It is false merely to blame our enemies, to point a finger at the obviously wicked, to clear our consciences by populating the other half of the world, in our minds, with devils. It is false, too, to shift the blame by Sunday morning quarterbacking the mistakes of our own leaders, for in a democracy, the actions of leaders must always in the end derive from the will of the people.

The opening of the year is a good time to look at ourselves broadly, and to ask ourselves just what our dedications are, and whether they are sufficient.

Up above I mentioned that in this country we still live in happiness, freedom, and comfort. I wonder what is the order of our dedication to these three things?

For instance, one of our greatest dedications should be to freedom, but are we so dedicated? Or are we by chance also dedicated to comfort, and that to such an extent that we seek to compromise between freedom and comfort, accepting a little less of the first in order to retain plenty of the second? Not a bad thing to think about hard. Comfort is almost totally material. It involves possessions, food, and such things. Comfort is connected with not paying heavy taxes, with not being annoyed, with butter before guns. It relates also to knowing that in a pinch the state, or someone, or something, will take care of you regardless of your deserts. Comfort forbids risks. Insecurity destroys comfort. We have fantastic comfort, compared to the world at large, and we should be grateful for it, but we must never let it become an end, an object of our dedication.

What about happiness? To say we have happiness is to say that we have freedom to pursue happiness, if we are capable of experiencing it and know what it is. The rest is up to us.

Happiness involves such things as the capacity of loving. It is in no way dependent upon comfort, as any saint could tell us, but it is absolutely dependent upon freedom, even upon that highest freedom through which men can of their own wills dedicate themselves and sacrifice themselves.

The founding fathers were not far off when they wrote of

"life, liberty, and the pursuit of happiness," in that order. Without the first two the third cannot be; and if the third is properly conceived, if men pursue those things which really will make men happy, then the three belong together, are parts of one whole, interdependent, inseparable. Taken thus, this ringing statement does not merely define human rights, it is a call to godliness.

This column is sounding like a sermon which I am in no way qualified to preach. I have written thus simply because these thoughts have been occurring and recurring to me these past six days, and they seem to have some relevance at the beginning of a new year in a time of stress and danger. True happiness must be a very great thing; it must take greatness to achieve it. It involves freedom, life, love, service, and faith.

The author of this piece is in no way great. At this moment, for obvious reasons, he is experiencing considerable happiness within his capacity, and so, with gratitude, and in the fullest, highest meaning of the phrase, he wishes everyone a Happy New Year.

Today, a year later, is our son's first birthday. The event is important to us, and to some of our friends, but not to the rest of the world nor to the child himself, who will probably try to eat the candle, hug the cake, and blow out his grandmother. A few years from now he will discover, what his father had to learn, that being born so close to Christmas is a gyp.

A year and a week ago, reading St. Luke aloud, the thought of our own child so soon to come gave the event special depth. That is true again this year, while the child still has the quality of a babe; one can't help making an analogy. Later, when the child can walk, say a few words, and generally act as a child,

he will enrich Christmas in a different way, providing the natural, only really right center for the whole celebration.

For some three months now, and for somewhat more than
three months to come, this infant is in the first period of enchantment. This is the period of lively response, utter innocence, and babyhood. Another high period of enchantment
comes a little later, when innocence is still whole and the
child possesses words in which he constantly reveals what we
are forever forgetting — that all the world is full of wonder.

The day will come, I trust, when on Christmas Day we'll
lift our cups of eggnog together, and his mother will borrow a
cigarette from him, and no doubt that period will also have
its rewards and parental satisfactions, but at the moment I
don't look forward to it with pleasure. One feels a curious
mixture of profoundly wishing one's child to grow and develop as all others do, and deep regret that it must happen.

These thoughts bring to mind that I also narrowly missed
being a Christmas baby. My mother had a good, solid,
healthy, Anglo-Saxon streak of sentimentality, and no doubt
half a century ago she indulged in thoughts about me similar
to those that I am setting down about this youngster. When
I think of the battered, aging, and peculiar image that confronts me when, of necessity, I stand up to the mirror to
shave, this realization rocks the mind. All one can do is hope
feebly that the son will be better than the father. At least,
facially better assembled, giving less the impression of having
been put together out of spare parts left over from one of
those long, New England genealogies.

Better, by far, to put the mind on the future in an impersonal way. After all, that is what the child, and I, too, for a
while yet, must live in. New Year's Day is coming up, and
columnists are supposed to get off something neatly appropriate. The Christmas–New Year's combination makes about

the pleasantest week of the whole year. The relaxation that sets in on Christmas Day, with all the shopping and wrapping and hiding and arranging and cooking and decorating done with, is a little like the calm after an election day in which everybody's candidate won.

There is the sense of continued holiday, a week in which Sunday very cleverly pops up in the middle. Work (including that involved in writing a column) is held to a minimum. The carry-over of good feeling runs through to the second holiday, and enables us once more to look upon the New Year as being full of promise rather than menace.

The child has come nicely through his vaccination, the cake looks nice, and there is sherry for the grownups. Everything that is less than thirty-six inches above the floor, that can be pulled loose, twisted, bitten through, or broken has been removed, and it is time to turn the lovely little monster loose. Yes indeed, things are looking up.

When the broom lies diagonally across the guest-room bed, on top of the monogrammed throw, with a copy of *Macbeth* beside it, and the dust-pan is on top of the third row of books in the bookshelf in the study;

When a can of shoe-polish, a big kitchen spoon, and the upper part of an aluminum double boiler that has obviously been used for pounding rocks lie together under a rose bush, while the lower part of the double boiler is in the wastebasket in the living room in the company with a cigarette holder and two unopened letters;

When the trowel is on the couch, the rake in the front hall across the doorway, and most of the remaining grass seed is in a tin cup in the sink, along with the heirloom silver fork that has been used to mix the seed with water and soap (the rest of the bar of kitchen soap having migrated to the hearth in the living room);

And the clothes that had been placed in the washing machine for washing are draped in part over the bedroom radiator, in part stuffed into empty places in the bookshelves, having been replaced in the washing machine by two broken pencils and a copper ashtray;

Or if you find the cover of the last number of *The New Yorker* neatly arranged as a tent over the dog's bowl of water, with the rest of that eminent publication reposing, moist, in the bathtub;

While one bathtowel lies in the armchair ordinarily reserved for the master of the house, with a copy of Bartlett's *Familiar Quotations* face down upon it, and another bathtowel will eventually turn up behind the overcoats in the closet in the hall;

When the master's Stetson reposes on the pillow in the bedroom, and the mistress' best Mexican rebozo is crumpled under the kitchen table; when there is water in the big ashtray, and a cigarette butt floats in the flower vase, and the dog's water bowl has been carefully washed with the best dishrag, wiped out with Kleenex, and set to dry beside the ivory, African figurine on the shelf over the radiator;

When the bucket for washing floors has been half filled with soapy water and stands in the doorway between the living room and the kitchen with the egg-beater in it, and from the bucket to the far end of the living room extend the loops and spirals of what was recently a new ball of string;

When (continuing the spiral motif), spirals have been drawn all over the routine, courtesy letter from the senior senator of the state that reposes on the desk of the study, and the letter has been punched full of small holes, as though it had fallen into the hands of an obsessed Republican;

When a dime has been firmly wedged between the wood and glass in the aperture of the radio where you read the numbers, and the slit of the piggy-bank is clogged with a Graham cracker;

When there is a poker in the front yard, a briar pipe on Madame's dressing table, an odd, triangular piece of wood on the couch, and three dry stems of hollyhock have been tastefully displayed upon the central Navaho rug while the Indian drum lies on its side under the dining table and the drumstick is on the desk beside the senator's letter;

And a sort of paper-chase trail of paper clips extends through all the bedrooms, the bath, and the connecting hall;

When a great many small things that are usually kept ready to hand in the kitchen have been placed upon the highest possible shelves, and the washing machine has been firmly tied with strong twine to the hot-water pipe in the corner;

When the mistress of the house keeps her powder and powder puff on a shelf so high that she herself must climb on a chair to get at it;

And when none of these circumstances, or all or any of them occurring at one time, repetitiously, or in sequence, surprise, discommode, or annoy any of the inhabitants of the house;

And when, not seeing the sieve on its hook in the kitchen, without further thought or any concern the lady of the house goes and gets it from under the apple tree in the garden, and the lord and master similarly retrieves his screwdriver from under the bathtub;

And when the dog is totally incapable of being surprised by anything whatsoever;

You may lay your money with comfortable assurance of winning that there is a healthy, intelligent, active two-and-a-half-year-old child in the house.

For years I have heard about people who had a green thumb, and never took much stock in it. Scientific training induces skepticism, and I could not bring myself to believe that flowers, shrubs, cornstalks or cabbages were responsive to personalities. Pretty some of them, yes; useful, others, distinctly; but appreciative of individuals, no.

The only magical influence I recognized derived from observations of my childhood, which was that elderly ladies who wear worn-out gloves and work with a basket of tools get remarkable results. Logical analysis of this belief in the light of scientific method led to the conclusion that this was so because such ladies have been gardening devotedly for many years and know all about it.

My views, in short, boiled down to an idea that if you knew enough and were careful enough, you could make things grow. The converse of which is the exasperated realization that people like myself, who garden occasionally, hurriedly, and usually in deep ignorance, do not make things grow. They must depend upon those particular plants that simply can't be ruined.

Now I am perturbed to find what seems to be an irrefutable case of green thumb right in my own household. This is upsetting. The next thing I know, I'll be foretelling the weather by the flight of birds and sowing certain grains in the dark of the moon. The case, the evidence of which I can no longer refute, is the Light of Our House and (I hope) the future Prop of Our Declining Years, also and not inaccurately known as Little Deplorable, now four years old.

Although in many ways a true Child of the Atomic Age, this Ray of Sunshine has latterly taken a deep interest in gardening, and likes to Help Daddy and Mummy. When helping takes the form of pulling a fine plant up by the roots, or aiming the hose at a half-opened window, one may be annoyed, but one is not surprised, but when it comes to feats of horticulture that defy competition, I give up.

Thus, at regular intervals I plant grass. I do it as per one of

Mr. Clark's columns — I think. I get about a 12 per cent crop. The Son and Heir, inevitably, also plants grass. He drops seed in great dollops, throws peat moss on top, and slings hunks of manure at it. (There is nothing the Growing Mind loves more than a manure mud pie.) He gets a 100 per cent crop. Find a rich, velvety island in our semi-desert — that's the work of the Child of the House.

By the same token, I plant a little corn, meticulously, by the directions, in rows I have painstakingly levelled. The Little Helper scratches a small pit off to one side, throws in nine grains, and covers them. Half of my hills produce one or two stalks apiece. His young jungle is all doing wonderfully. This kind of thing is upsetting, even infuriating.

The hydrant in our garden can be cut off for winter by an iron handle sunk in the ground. The hole in which it is sunk is lined with four boards. For some weeks prior to the planting season, the Young Gardener occupied himself with raising the level of this hole by dropping in, alternately, sand, adobe, leaves, several marbles, plain dirt, two red stones, and fragments of a celluloid toy.

A friend gave us some onion sets. We (adults) planted most of them in the usual manner, and with reasonably successful results. The Son and Heir glommed onto a handful of the extras for his own uses, which we took to be of a missile nature. About two weeks ago he insisted I come and see what he had growing in "the wooden hole." It appeared to be a fine, healthy onion. I insisted he'd pulled it out of the onion patch and dropped it there, so he had to pull it up to prove to me that it was rooted in situ. Of course that finished the onion, which was my fault.

I give up. Next spring I shall hand him all our seeds and a large spoon and let him take charge. That way we may get some results, and a number of interesting surprises.

*

Something, I don't know what, woke me early Friday morning. Even before I opened my eyes, I knew that it had *snew*. It was the almost feral intuition of an old outdoorsman who in his prime roamed the primeval forests (also in their prime) and sandy deserts from New England to Central America. There is a quality in the air after snowfall, a freshness, that is unmistakable.

My ability thus to determine the state of nature outside a window covered by drawn curtains was not hampered, of course, by the fact that I had seen it snowing the evening before. A good outdoorsman takes advantage of all those little aids, just as he puts kerosene on the firewood if he has any handy and reads the road signs as well as studying the trail.

It was also reasonably apparent that it had turned mighty cold, so it occurred to me as a good idea to take a look into the child's room and see that he was covered. The very young sleep soundly, and sometimes they toss out of the blankets, especially after knocking off a whale of a Thanksgiving dinner, on top of an orgy of high-class Chinese food at Shuster's birthday party Wednesday. Now I think of it, maybe it was that combination that had me alert, briefly in the stilly dark, after a rather complex dream.

As I pottered about, turning up the heat a little, looking out at the snow, checking the Son and Heir, my mind picked up where it had left off earlier, wrestling with the idea of Thanksgiving itself. The matter had been plaguing me for some days.

Exactly what are we giving thanks for this year? The world is a horrid mess, strewn with such mass suffering and oppression that the imagination fails, threatening us with tragedy at any moment. Our leaders falter, fumble, take vacations.

Here, inside our own borders, we are fairly comfortable. In places, hatred verging on insanity bombs schools to prevent our acting like Christians. In places, the battle to keep every

tenth American in a state of subjection is being bitterly
fought. There is sorrow and suffering in this country, too.
Ask the Indians of the Plains region.

But you and I are comfortable, and so far we are safe. We
have worldly goods. As a nation, we were never better off;
probably no large nation in all history has been as well fed,
housed, clothed, and motorized, by and large, as are we today. Is that what we should give thanks for? Or should we
not perhaps look upon this material wealth with mistrust,
fearing that it may so soften us that in the end we shall be-
tray ourselves merely to postpone discomfort?

Is it not in deference to this very softness that our President
himself works to reduce yet further our armed forces in order
to balance the budget?

For what shall I give thanks? I was worrying about it again
as I turned my flashlight into the little boy's room and saw
that he did not need to be covered.

Then it occurred to me that to be elderly and to have a
child in the house not quite seven, to make Thanksgiving, to
make Christmas, the Fourth of July, the burning of Zozobra,
was no small blessing. And if this be so, then the very fact
that we still have a little space, some strength, some time,
some friends, indeed millions of people of goodwill standing
with us against the enemy, thinking of the future, of children,
is a most profound cause for giving thanks. With this I has-
tened back to bed.

Not very deep thinking, perhaps, but anyway, even before
I opened my eyes I knowed it had snowed.

Christmas is a strange confusion. Beginning in October,
our mail begins to fill with catalogues; at times it seems as if
Christmas itself, generosity, warmth, had been drowned in
the cries of the hucksters. At times it seems as if its deeper

essence had been overwhelmed by the pleasures of the feast. It is an occasion of a thousand meanings.

How must a child of four figure it? When I question The Menace, I get an impression of glorified practicality. There will be things, there will be Santa Claus, there will be delicious foods, and yet even to the down-to-earth infant mind, one sees, a greater quality is apparent. The Christ story begins to take hold, he can at least be subjected to St. Luke's account, but the interpretation is primitive, and St. Nicholas still is dominant.

A child's world is a strange one. It is full of conflicts and incongruities that would terrify an adult, and the child accepts them calmly, with extraordinary elasticity of mind. Our Christmas tradition has its roots deeply in northern Europe, and carries over many references and vestiges that adults accept metaphorically; but a child is literal. In the American centuries, it still looks to the north and dreams of snow, deep snow, but in New Orleans they sit on their balconies and listen to the firecrackers.

Our culture has changed so fast that traditions cannot possibly keep up with it. The air is full of a debased, truncated version of "Jingle Bells" — and how many of my readers, I wonder, have ridden in a sleigh? We tell of nightcaps, the pictures show four-poster beds, and a child's literature is full of steam engines and clocks that tick and strike. We run to inaudible wrist watches, silent electric clocks, and I don't remember when I last heard a clock strike or saw a pendulum swing. Where can I take a child today to see a first-rate steam engine, how justify "choo-choo"? It even takes some searching to find a cow being milked by hand.

Our own immediate pasts have become a part of fairy land, and the co-operative infants accept it, visualize it — I wonder just how — dwell in it. The other day we had our Little

Problem write a letter to Santa Claus, and I confidently put it in the flames, so that he could see it go up the chimney. Our chimney won't draw up a shred of paper. This is a sign of some sort. Even the climate is changing, and what we used to laugh at as old men's tales is now scientific fact — the chances of a white Christmas grow slimmer yearly.

"The answer to all of which," said the Man with the Calabash Pipe, reading shamelessly over my shoulder, "is, relax! Perhaps you cannot explain to that infant over whom you are so besotted that the angels didn't say 'Peace on earth, good will to men' but 'to men of good will,' and perhaps you can't show off by pointing out the significance and realism of that declaration. What of it? What if the tale of Bethlehem is still, to him, just one of many stories? That doesn't mean he takes it lightly; he takes them all seriously. His time for shedding them will come — then you can worry lest he shed too much."

Having demolished my chain of thought, he sat down in my armchair. "As for the child, little by little," he said between puffs at his pipe. "As for you adults, give thanks. You still have the pure acceptance of wonder, you still have a pair of eyes through which you can at least get a glimpse of what Christmas once was to you. Accept the delight while it is offered to you. And by all means read him St. Luke. He won't understand it, but it will help train his ear. Pass me the matches, please."